The History of Lancashire Cookery

by

Tom Bridge Master Chef

PRINTWISE PUBLICATIONS LIMITED
1992

All recipes in this book © Tom Bridge

© Printwise Publications 1992

Published by Printwise Publications Ltd.,
47 Bradshaw Road, Tottington, Bury, Lancs, BL8 3PW.

Warehouse and Orders:
40-42 Willan Industrial Estate, Vere Street,
(off Eccles New Road),
Salford, M5 2GR.
Tel: 061-745 9168
Fax: 061-737 1755

ISBN No. 1 872226 25 6

Edited by

Cliff Hayes

Front cover drawing by Gerry Halpin of Rivington Fine Arts.
Tel. 0257 483406

Printed and bound by Manchester Free Press,
Paragon Mill, Jersey Street,
Manchester, M4 6FP
Tel: 061-236 8822

**THIS BOOK IS DEDICATED
TO THE MEMORY OF
ANN O'NEIL.**

INTRODUCTION

Having worked very hard in the profession of cookery for over 25 years I was presented in March 1991 with a 'Plaq d'Or' from the World Master Chefs Society by H.R.H. The Princess Royal whom I have had the pleasure of meeting on several occasions. During our brief conversation we talked with regards to my books on Cookery and my background in the North of England. It was then that Her Royal Highness The Princess Anne suggested: and when am I going to be able to read a book written by yourself on the History of Lancashire Cookery.

So it is to H.R.H. The Princess Royal that I give my personal thanks for the title of this book. It is also to The Princess Royal's dearest cause that I am making a donation from the royalties to the SAVE THE CHILDREN FUND.

Princess Anne who for twenty years has confronted famine and disease in the poorest regions of the world for SAVE THE CHILDREN FUND I hope will delight in knowing that people buying the book will have contributed to this cause.

Tom Bridge being presented to H.R.H. The Princess Royal

BUCKINGHAM PALACE

4 September 1991

Dear Mr Bridge,

The Princess Royal has asked me to thank you for your letter dated 30th August, 1991.

Her Royal Highness remembers well her conversation with you at Claridges and is delighted that your book has been published and accepts your kind offer on behalf of the Save the Children Fund of 50% of the royalties.

The address of the Save the Children Fund is:

The Director General,
The Save the Children Fund,
Mary Datchelor House,
17 Grove Lane,
London, SE5 8RH.

Her Royal Highness sends you her sincere thanks for your kind donation to the Strathcarron Hospice and conveys to you her very best wishes.

Lieutenant Colonel Peter Gibbs, LVO
Private Secretary to
HRH The Princess Royal

Tom Bridge, Esq.

Save the Children

REGISTERED OFFICE
THE SAVE THE CHILDREN FUND
MARY DATCHELOR HOUSE
17 GROVE LANE
CAMBERWELL
LONDON SE5 8RD
TELEPHONE: 071-703 5400

NH/SB ·

19 September 1991

Mr Tom Bridge

Dear Mr Bridge

Thank you for your letter of 18 September and a copy of your enticing recipe collection, *The Heritage of Northern Cookery*. I have asked a colleague who deals with such fundraising matters to be in touch as soon as possible. May I take this opportunity of thanking you for your support of The Save the Children Fund.

Nicholas Hinton

C:\WS2000\LETTER\NH-19.SEP
Telegrams & Cables: Savinrana London SE5.   Telex No. 892809 SCFLON G.   Fax No. 071-703 2278 (G3)
A company registered in London No. 178159 and limited by guarantee.   Registered Charity No. 213890.
Patron Her Majesty The Queen.   President: Her Royal Highness The Princess Royal, GCVO.
Chairman: Viscount Boyd.   Hon. Treasurer: Mr. W. H. Yates, F.R.I.C.S.   Director General: Nicholas Hinton, C.B.E.

ABOUT THE AUTHOR

I was born in the Lancashire Mill Town of Bolton and I must have been about eight years old when I first became interested in cooking, though at the time I did not imagine just what my interest would lead to in the future.

I remember coming home from school, or from football or swimming, and finding my mother in our big kitchen busily baking, boiling or roasting? I would be at one end of the big table kneading plasticine-like lumps of dough on my mother's marble pastry board. Mother would be at the other end of the table vigorously stirring her savoury mincemeat for her mince pies. Two of my specialities in those days were Lancashire Scones and Jam Fritters.

As time went on I became better and better at cooking, enjoying it more and more, and to my delight was allowed to do my share of the family baking: though I never succeeded in making a Tatie Pie like Mothers.

When I was fourteen I decided that I would not be a professional footballer or open the batting for Lancashire, but I would become a chef. I was a real Jack-the-lad, and school was not my favourite subject. After a few strokes on the backside from Billy Hall and Derek Billington at Brownlow Fold High School in Bolton, I went to work at the Commercial Hotel, which is now where Mothercare stands in Bolton precinct. I washed beer bottles and peeled vegetables for a great man called Abe Scott the Landlord, who was always clipping me about the ear-hole for watching the chefs at work.

Fannie & Johnnie Cradock and Philip Harben were television celebrities, when I was young, and I studied in great detail their books and watched their television programmes. Needless to say, I was promoted at 16 to commis chef and my career began, thanks to their lessons.

My first big dinner, I remember, was in 1976 when I was executive chef at the National Liberal Club in Whitehall, London, it was for Dr. Donald Coggan, then Archbishop of Canterbury. Jeremy Thorpe and Cyril Smith, now Sir Cyril, were also there. I did Trout in Almonds, and after the meal Jeremy Thorpe brought Dr. Coggan into the kitchen. Just at that moment I had a basket of bread rolls in my hand, and Dr. Coggan said "Chef, the fish was wonderful" and quick to wit, I said "Well what about the loaves SIR?" (fishes and loaves from the bible)....., a burst of laughter was followed by Stilton and Vintage Port.

I then worked for various people on a free-lance basis, several high ranking politicians and celebrities. Writing a diet sheet for Frank Sinatra, cooking over 150,000 meals in one week during Live Aid. Organising 20,000 bacon rolls for the George Michael and Andrew Ridgley 'Wham' Finale at Wembley to setting a Reebok shoe in ice, and creating ice carvings for Charlton Heston and Jane Seymour. I wrote a sporting fit plan, which educates them into what are the best foods to eat and what the dangerous foods are, (did me no good I am three stone overweight).

H.R.H. Prince Andrew said of my Noisettes of Lamb "Baaa" he liked them cooked pink. I have taught English Cookery to the Chinese in San Francisco, and was taught Italian Cookery in Portugal by a Frenchman, made Lancashire Hot Pot and Irish Soda Bread in Ireland for golfers' Tony Jacklin and Severiano Ballesteros at Woodbrook in Bray. The most unusual thing I ever did was to cook English food for a large party of Europeans in the Wyoming/Denver valley all on horse-back for a full 14 days.

My first cookery book *The People of Bolton on Cookery* was described as "fascinating reading" by the late Reg. Barker in the *Cater and Hotelkeeper*. This then set me on the road of writing, and since I have written several books on the History of Cookery. My favourite Hotel is the Sharrow Bay Country House Hotel, Lake Ullswater near Pooley Bridge in Penrith. My favoutite food is LBT's (lettuce, bacon and tomato toasted sandwiches). My favourite chef is John Benson Smith, he has that touch of eccentricity that is needed to promote food, he is very gifted and unconventional.

My favourite pastime is going for long walks with my wife Jayne and my boys Gareth and Matthew around the beautiful village of Newburgh, where we live. The highlight of my career to date is being presented with the Haute Cuisine Plaq d'Or for my work in catering at Claridges in London by H.R.H. The Princess Royal on behalf of the World Master Chefs Society in March 1991. And the Epicurian Mondial Gold Medal from the President of the World Master Chefs Society, my dear friend, Master Chef and Author, Jean Conil.

ACKNOWLEDGEMENTS

To the Princess Royal for her initial suggestion, and to Nicolas Hinton CBE, Director General of the Save the Children Fund for his help.

Rosemary Bromely my Literary Agent in Hampshire for her very sound help and advice.

Paula & Bob Yoxall, The Royal Clifton Hotel, Southport for bringing Jayne and myself together.

The English Tourist Board, David Hewitt, Jack Hampson, Bill & Steven Thornley and all the staff at Thornley's Pork Products, at Ridgewood Farm, Flag Lane, Heath Charnock in Chorley; Ron & Lorraine Lambton at Maxim's of Bolton. Marc McCrone.

The Generosity of the people of Newburgh and the PTA.

Colin Cooper-English, Paul Yeo & David Little for their Advice.

Madge & Bill Croft for reminding me I am only human.

Connie Denton & Jim O'Neil & family for being good neighbours.

Yvonne & Simon Wildi, Gaynor & Tony Wigley.

Julie Benson & Wyn Godfrey at The Walnut Tree in Bootle.

Jim Fitzpatrick & Mary Whittle, Dave Cross, Marie & Martin Chesterfield. Pat Cobham & Keith Jenkins at CM Associates in Liverpool, Phil Berry, Derek & Andrea Hulse, Robert White, Martin & Maureen Marsh, Richard Underwood, Derek Billington, John Sherry, Andy Britton , Richard Groves, Graham Blakeway, Sarah Pudge, Bill Moreland, Reg Syddal, Jean Tomlinson, Phil Walsh, George & Francis Saint, Neil Foster, Christine Dawson, Kathryn Southern, Beth Dunster, Veronica Scott, Cheryl & Norah Middleton, Nicola McPherson, Ryan and the twins. Jeremy Rata, The Preston Crest Hotel, Peter Smith at The Red Lion Hotel, Newburgh.

Dave Lonsdale, Rose & Dave at The Edge Tavern for being old.

Jayne Ellis-Bridge for being the perfect woman, while I compiled this monstrosity.

Finally Cliff Hayes and all the staff at Printwise Publications Ltd and everyone involved with the book who I have missed out, you have not been forgotten.

OTHER BOOKS BY TOM BRIDGE

"The People of Bolton on Cookery"

"The Golden Age of Cookery"

"Lancashire Recipes Old and New"

Being published soon

"Great Cookery Writers of England"

"A Regency Eccentric/ Southover Press"

"National Television"

"The Kitchen Craft Club"

"Bridge over Britain"

Contents

Chapter 1

ELIZABETH RAFFALD
1733-1781
THE MOTHER OF NORTHERN
ENGLISH COOKERY

This remarkable lady Elizabeth Raffald was the daughter of Joshua Whittaker of Doncaster, and was born in 1733. I am only going to give you a very brief history on this lady, because very soon you can read and watch on Channel 4 television her complete life story for which I am still doing the research.

She was destined to become one of the most fascinating ladies of the eighteenth century. After receiving a fair education, in 1748 she went into private service for fifteen years, her last employer being Lady Elizabeth Warburton at Arley Hall in Cheshire which you can still visit today. And like myself Arley Hall has one of the very few original copies of her wonderful book *The Experienced English Housekeeper*.

Here she met and married the head gardener of Arley Hall, John Raffald in 1763. The couple moved to Manchester, and John Raffald joined his brothers in a florist and market gardening business run from a market stall, whilst his wife Elizabeth opened up a confectioner's shop in Fennel Street, Manchester.

It was the very hard training that Elizabeth had received in private service which stood her in good stead for all her later business activities. Her husband John was not made of the same stern stuff. His love of 'ardent spirits' led him all too frequently to the gin shop and the fallen woman, before long his own business failed. During the next eighteen years, Elizabeth produced (like a factory) sixteen daughters. Though virtually pregnant all her married life, this remarkable lady started on a business venture that was to change her life dramatically.

With her currant drops, white plum cakes & ratafia cakes the confectionery shop prospered. She was the first of her kind in the north to give cookery lesson's and opened probably the first servants registry office (catering agency) in Manchester.

In here book and a notice dated 1764, announces her entry into business.

Just arrived, and now selling wholesale and retail, at Mrs Raffalds in Fennel Street, fine Canterbury and Derbyshire Brawn whole, half a quarter collars of the Canterbury grown at 16d the pound, and those of Derby shire 14d the pound.

As several of Mrs Raffalds friends in the country have mistook her Terms & Designs of her Registry Office, she begs leave to inform them that she supplies Families with servants, at any distance, at ONE shilling each.

Masters and servants, therefore, at any distance, may be supplied on the shortest notice, by directing (Post Paid) to Mrs Raffald at the REGISTER OFFICE in Fennel Street, Manchester.

She also continues to supply families with made dishes, cold suppers & c., as usual (*Could this be the first English Take Away?*).

This lady had without doubt a very original mind way ahead of her time. Good servants where very hard to find and she founded a company to recruit staff and today staff recruitment agencies are everywhere.

The servants agency was new, and like all innovations it attracted at first a great deal of ridicule. In August 1764, numerous jokes about the agency were being reflected from the stage. A theatre bill in that month advertise:

Following the first Part of King Henry IVth, with the Humours of Sir John Falstaff, scene taken from the REGISTER OFFICE, 'and to which is added a farce called THE INTRIGUING CHAMBERMAID'.

It was in that year that Elizabeth Raffald made her personality well known in the prosperous and growing city of Manchester. It grew rapidly. In 1757 the population was nineteen thousand eight hundred. In 1775 when the next census was taken it reached a peak of twenty eight thousand which was a very large figure for the time and like the city, Elizabeth Raffald also expanded. The shop was very successful and within a year had increased her little take-away into the first supermarket in Britain. She now sold Yorkshire Hams, Rolled Salmon, cooked Rabbits, PORTABLE SOUP (*Who said Soyer started the soup kitchens?*) Tongues, Potted meats, pickles, bread, cheese, Mushroom Catchup, sweetmeats and all kinds of made dishes, that without doubt started life as traditional northern fare.

She was a very enterprising woman of the highest degree. She superintended arrangements for public and private dinners and was well known for these achievements. She took the Bull's Head Inn in the market place and ran that so well that the officers of the regiments stationed at Manchester had their mess table at the Bull's Head, and on her removal to the King's Head, Salford, the officers' mess moved also.

The shop at the corner of Old Exchange Alley is no longer there, but the Bull's Head Inn in the Market Place was still there until 1930. Her cookery book appeared in 1769 and young married ladies would say, ''I have got Mrs. Raffalds book, and I would not be without.''

Elizabeth Raffald died on April 9th, 1781, while bearing her fifteenth child at the tender age of forty-eight, and was buried in Stockport Parish Church

For your interest I have ended each chapter with one of Mrs Elizabeth Raffalds famous northern recipes.

Chapter 2

FAVOURITE NORTHERN FARE

The Battle of the Roses was fought with vegence and still is at Old Trafford, but the one thing us Northerners have in common is the Great British Breakfast, no fruit juice, grapefruit, or croissants for us.

In my great grandfather's day it would have been bread, cheese and ale. Game was also seen regularly in nineteenth century northern homes, the table would have a Game Pie, although tea was introduced into England in the year of the Great Fire of London (1666), and has become the universal beverage of the people, the poor of the north, either did not know how to use it or preferred ale. Coffee was brought into England before tea. It was introduced by a servant of Mr.Edwards, a Smyrna (tobacco & figs) merchant in 1653, again the expense forbade us northerners even that until around the 1900s. According to Mary Jewry who wrote *Warnes Model Cookery* 1868, this is how to set up the breakfast table.

"At the head of the table place the breakfast cups and saucers, the tea cups at the left hand side, the coffee cups at the right hand. The teapot and coffee-pot stand in front of the urn. The slop-basin and milk-jug should be placed on the left.

The cream and hot milk to the right.

Put hot plates by the broiled bacon, chops and a smaller plate, knife and fork to each person. Bread should be put on a wooden platter. Salt-cellars occupy the four corners. Hot rolls should be brought in covered with a table napkin. Dry toast should never stand longer than five minutes before serving.

Buttered toast becomes soppy and greasy if too long kept before it is served. Large joints, as cold ham, cold beef, &c., should be put on the sideboard or a side table".

This not being the case in the north at all, the simplicity of our table would be, a table (scrubbed), salt and a mug of ale, Cold York Ham or some form of Game bird, pie or sausage with crusty bread. In the North of Scotland they have the traditional Arbroath Smokies, Kippers, Bloaters and Finnan Haddock.

What is the great North divide well I am hear to tell you it is the sausage, the institution for which the north is known the Pork Sausage, Cumberland sausage & Black Pudding.

The people of England eat over 20,000,000 sausages a day. And without doubt we have the edge over the rest of Britain when it comes to making a really good quality English Breakfast.

In the 1950's I watched television with my family and we used to watch this little lion appear and, then the phrase 'Go to work on an egg'. Now they were eggs! No mention of 'Sam & Ella' or that dreaded word 'Curry'. We were lucky! A fat, brown, farmhouse, new-laid, three and three quarter minute, boiled egg. Not quite so large, perhaps, as an ostrich egg, but considerably bigger than those small, stale, white horrors imported from goodness knows where.

And as we, in company with millions of our fellow country people, happily go to work on our morning eggs, don't we feel sorry for all the millions of people in Spain & Italy and other countries, who go to work on only a small cup of coffee.... and a Scooter? What about the succulence of York Ham lightly grilled with fried eggs, Grilled slices of black pudding, rounds of succulent cumberland sausage, fried bread, tomatoes topped with HP sauce.

Here are some of the popular northern breakfast recipes of yester-year.

BACON FRITTERS
(Ann O'Neil, Newburgh)

During the time of rationing every subterfuge had to be discovered to make bacon go as far as possible. Here is one of them.

Roll up some thin rashers of lean bacon, tie them with string, parboil them, and let them go cold. Untie them then dip them in a good coating of batter and fry them in dripping.

I remember Dripping on Toast for tea with cocoa !

BACON PANCAKES
(Ian Bentley, Liverpool)

Cut up some grilled bacon rashers in very small pieces. Make some pancake batter and when it is ready, add the bacon seasoning well, frying the pancakes in the usual way.

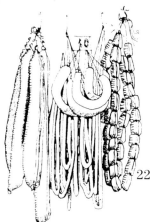

LANCASHIRE RABBIT
(Ron & Lorraine Lambton, Bolton)

225g (8 oz) Grated Lancashire Cheese
2 tablespoons of cream
4 slices of Warburtons Bread
1 tablespoon English mustard

Blend the cheese, cream and mustard together in a bowl. Toast one side of the bread and then spoon the cheese mixture over the untoasted side, top with slices of tomato. Put the bread under a hot grill and cook until the cheese is brown.

I like to add slices of tomato, when I make this recipe

And now this is a secret let out after 91 years — the far famed 'Bury Black Pudding' of which I have promised not to give the weights involved. So now you know the ingredients of the famed pudding but alas you still will not be able to make them.

The Far-Famed
BURY BLACK PUDDING

Take groats and pearl barley, tie up loosely in a bag and boil until cooked, place in a large tub and add seasoning, flour and onions chopped. Mix well whilst hot. Add back fat or leaf cut into quarter inch square. Now add blood and stiffen with oatmeal.

Fill into bullock runners with pudding filler, allowing about 6 to 8 pieces of fat to each pudding. Tie up firmly and boil gently for about 20 minutes.

Slice and serve with mustard or allow them to cool, slice and grill them serve with fried egg.

The method for Black Pudding in the north was a little different in 1811. I do suggest that you do not even attempt this recipe.

BLACK PUDDINGS
(The Frugal Housewife, Manchester 1811)

Before you kill a hog get a peck of groats, boil them half an hour in water, then drain them, and put them in a clean tub or large pan.

Then kill your hog, save two quarts of the blood, and keep stirring it till it is quite cold; then mix it with your groats, and stir them well together. Season with a large teaspoon of salt, a quarter of an ounce of cloves, mace, and nutmeg together, an equal quantity of each; dry it, beat it well, and mix in.

Take a little winter savoury, sweet-marjoram and thyme, penny-royal stripped of the stalks and chopped very fine; just enough to season them, and give them flavour, but no more.

The next day take the leaf of the hog, and cut it into dice, scrape, and wash the guts very clean, then tie one end, and begin to fill them, but be sure to put in a good deal of fat, fill the skins three parts full, tie the other end, and make your puddings what length you please; prick them with a pin, and put them in a kettle of boiling water. boil them slowly for an hour, then take them out, lay them on clean straw.

I had a visit to Thornley's in Chorley and watched with glee, the making of this very unique Lancashire speciality and I still enjoy having them fried for breakfast and boiled, served with English mustard for my supper.

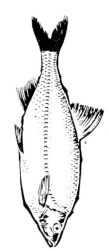

BREAKFAST ROLLS
(Mary Jewry 1868)
converted by author

450g (1lb) flour
125g (8oz) butter
15ml (1 tbsp) yeast
1 fresh egg
150ml (5fl oz) warm milk

Rub the butter into the flour, then add the yeast, breaking in one egg, both yolk and white. Mix it with a little warm milk poured into the middle of the flour; stir all well together, and set it by a fire to rise, (cover with a warm cloth and leave in a warm area for 30 minutes), then make it into alight dough. Cut into rolls, lay them on a tin, and set them in front of the fire for ten minutes before you put them into th oven, brushing them over with egg. This paste may be used for fancy bread. *Author's Note: Place into a Moderate Oven Gas 5, 375f for 15-20 minutes.*

BLOATER FILLETS ON TOAST
(Master Chef Noel Emms)

Simmer the bloaters in hot water for three minutes, then skin and fillet them. Brush the fillets over with a little butter, sprinkle them with freshly ground black pepper, put each on a slice of butter toast and bake in the oven for a few minutes.

SCRAMBLED EGGS WITH LANCASHIRE CHEESE
(Jayne Ellis-Bridge)

Nobody can do this like my missus, she like Francis Coulson is one of the best Breakfast cooks I have ever met. They should be soft and slightly runny.

The eggs, usually three per person, are beaten and lightly seasoned with freshly ground black pepper with a little cream and three ounces of grated Lancashire cheese.

Melt a knob of butter in a small (non-stick) pan, when thoroughly melted pour in the eggs. Cook over a low heat, stirring well with a wooden spoon. Just before the eggs begin to set serve on toast.

N.B: Jayne usually takes the eggs off when they are slightly runny, as they continue cooking for a further 30 seconds without heat.

Bread crumbs
2 egg yolks
100gm (4 ozs) butter
300ml (10 fl oz) good gravy
salt & pepper

Parboil the ears for half an hour. Make a forcemeat of the sage, onion, finely chopped suet, breadcrumbs, pepper and salt. Mix and bind it with beaten egg yolks. Raise the skin of the upper sides of the ears, and stuff them with it. Fry the ears in fresh butter to a nice brown colour. Pour away the fat and drain them well.
Place in the gravy and cook them over a fire for half hour. Serve with fresh parsley.

Authors note: Having experimented with this very unusual recipe, I can highly recommend it. These can quite easily be obtained from any of the Thornley Pork shops through-out the north, who I am very grateful for their support in supplying me with informative material & food products for my experiments.

PIGS EARS
dedicated to David Hewitt
(Thornley's, Chorley.)

This was also used for a main meal in the poor houses of the north in the 1800s, but was one of the most attractive dishes in the household of the gentry

2 Ears
Sage & Onion 100g (4 ozs)
Suet 50g (2 oz)

16

LANCASHIRE COUNTRY EGGS
(Michael & Gaynor Chesterfield)

This recipe was given to me by a true Lancashire man, who has this breakfast dish with a Pint of Real Ale.

Fry off half pound of bacon, then cut into small pieces placing them into a shallow oven- proof dish. Put a little dripping into the same pan and fry off some small cubes of raw potato, add these with the bacon. season them with a little pepper and break three eggs on top, adding finally a quarter of a pound of chopped mushrooms, place into the oven and bake until set.

EGGS BAKED IN BACON RINGS
SERVED WITH KEDGEREE
(Gaynor Black, Southport)

This recipe was given to me by a very dear old girl, who used to make this for her husband Tony's breakfast when she first got married.

Grill some bacon rashers partly, and put each into a muffin tin.
Break an egg into each, and bake in a moderate oven for about ten minutes. Serve at once on buttered toasts.
Served with kidneys and Kedgeree.

TONY WIGLEY'S KEDGEREE

This recipe is over 200 years old and is still very popular in the Stockport, Greater Manchester area when they used to use cold turbot or brill. Today they use finnan haddock or sardines which are plentiful and cheap.

Use equal quantities of cold finnan haddock and rice, with 2 ounces of best butter or margarine.
With one teaspoonful of mixed pepper, salt, and a little Cayenne, mince up the finnan haddock. Boil the same quantity of rice for 10 minutes. Put 50g (2 oz) of butter into a large frying pan, when hot toss in the fish & rice, seasoning well and serve with little lemon slices & fresh sprigs of parsley.

HAMS THE YORKSHIRE WAY
(The Young Woman's Companion 1811)

I have tried this recipe which takes three weeks, but I assure you will have great pleasure in serving this to your guests, knowing you have taken the time and effort to do it.

Mix well together half a peck of salt, three ounces of salt-petre, half an ounce of sal-prunella, and five pounds of very coarse salt. Rub the hams well with this: put them into a large pan or pickling tub, and lay the remainder on top. Let them lay three days, and then hang them up. Put as much water to pickle as will cover the hams, adding salt till it will bear an egg, and then boil and strain it. The next morning put in the hams, and press them down so they may be covered. Let them lay a fortnight, then rub them well with bran, and dry them.

The quantity of ingredients here directed is for doing three middle size hams at once, so that if you do only one, you must proportion the quantity of each article.

EGGS BAKED WITH YORK HAM
(Mr & Mrs Peter Radcliffe, Parbold)

Two friends of mine, Yvonne & Simon, remember their mothers curing Hams the Lancashire way, which was rubbed with sugar, saltpetre, salt, bay salt and pepper, they where then rubbed every day with the above mixture for three weeks in front of a warm fire.

Butter a shallow oven proof dish, and lay some thin slices of ham in the bottom. Break an egg on each slice of ham, and bake in the oven until the eggs are done.

This was then served with home-made brown bread or Hovis

YORK HAM SPREAD TOASTS
(Maureen & Martin Marsh)

225g (8 oz) Cooked York Ham,
chopped & pounded (mince)
25g (1 oz) softened butter
50g (2 oz) Scottish Cheddar
4 eggs, beaten
Freshly ground black pepper
4 slices of Hovis, toasted and butter (hot)

Into a large non-stick saucepan, blend the eggs, ham, butter, cheese and ground black pepper, Cook slowly stirring all the time for about 4 minutes until the consistency is creamy and thick.
Place enough on each piece of toast to completely cover and grill for 1 minute.

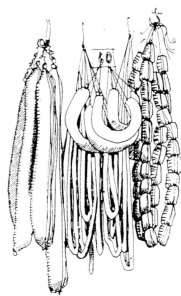

CUMBERLAND SAUSAGE

The traditional recipe for Cumberland sausage is made in several areas of the north besides Cumbria. It is far cheaper today to buy them from your butcher, than to even attempt to make them yourself, but for the experience, if you could afford to make them here are two traditional recipes.

(The Frugal Housewife 1811)

Take six pounds of young pork, free from skin, gristles and fat.
Cut it very small, and beat it in a mortar till it is very fine.
The shred six pounds of pork suet very fine and free from all skin. Take a good deal of sage, wash it very clean, and pick off the leaves, and shred it fine. Spread your meat on a clean dresser or table, and then shake the sage all over it, to the quantity of about three large spoonfuls. Shred the thin rind of a middling lemon very fine, and throw them over the meat, and also as many sweet herbs as, when shred fine, will fill a large spoon. Grate over it two nutmegs and put to it two tea-spoonfuls of pepper, and a large spoonful of salt. Then throw over it the suet, and mix all well together. Put it all down close in a pot, and when you use it, roll it up with as much egg as will make it roll smooth. Make them of the size of a sausage, and fry them in butter, or good dripping. Be careful the butter is hot before you put them in, and keep rolling them about while they are doing. When they are thoroughly hot, and of a fine light brown, take them out, put them into a dish, and serve them up. Veal mixed with pork, and done in this manner, eats exceedingly fine.

Elizabeth Raffald (1794)

This gives you an idea of how sausages were served and a recipe written in the years when George III was on the throne and George IV was Prince Regent. *(The letter f symbolises in some words the letter S).*

Cut them in fingle links, and fry them in frefh butter, then take a flice of bread, and fry it a good brown in the butter you fried the faufages in, and lay it in the bottom of your difh, put the faufages on the toaft, in four parts, and lay poached eggs betwixt them; pour a little good melted butter round them, and ferve them up.

Another traditional recipe give 4 parts of lean pork to 2 parts belly pork and 1 part back fat, seasoned well minced with rosemary, thyme & sage, with white pepper, cayenne, nutmeg & salt.

EGGS IN SHELLS
(Dave Cross, Merseyside)

Make a good white sauce, preferably with some cheese and chopped finnan haddock in it. Chop up finely some hard-boiled eggs, mixed with the sauce, put the mixture in scallop shells, sprinkle with some lightly browned bread crumbs and heat through in the oven, serve with fingers of toast.

Dave tells me this was very popular in Liverpool during the war.

EGGS BAKED WITH CUMBERLAND SAUSAGE
(Avril Cooper English)

Bake one pound of Cumberland sausage in a oven dish, after fifteen minutes, take them out and slice them thinly, keeping them warm.
Break six eggs into the dish, cover them with fine breadcrumbs and bake for four minutes.

BOLOGNA SAUSAGE
(Mary Jewry 1868)

Another taste of the north, this popular sausage which is now commonly known as Polony

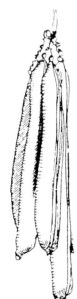

One Pound of beef
one pound of bacon
one pound of pork
one pound of beef suet
twelve sage leaves
a few sweet herbs
pepper and salt

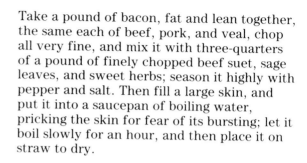

Take a pound of bacon, fat and lean together, the same each of beef, pork, and veal, chop all very fine, and mix it with three-quarters of a pound of finely chopped beef suet, sage leaves, and sweet herbs; season it highly with pepper and salt. Then fill a large skin, and put it into a saucepan of boiling water, pricking the skin for fear of its bursting; let it boil slowly for an hour, and then place it on straw to dry.

HADDOCK TAMS BRIGG
(Author)

Having worked a great deal in the North of Scotland several years ago, I heard of luxury breakfasts of Cold Sheep's Head, Rounds of Beef, Duck eggs served with Reindeer Ham, Smoked Salmon & marmalade, Haggis and Black pudding fried, with Kippers & Haddock smoked over oak chips.
This recipe is more popular today in the North West than any other area of England.

2 Finnan haddocks, each weighing
about 275g (10 oz)
Ground black pepper
2 eggs (uncooked)
2 eggs, hard boiled and finely chopped
25g (1 oz) butter
300ml (half pint) fresh milk
25g (1 oz) plain flour
1 pinch of tarragon
15ml (1 tbsp) chopped parsley

Into a large frying pan put the milk and ground black pepper, with a pinch of tarragon, place the haddock, skin side down

and bring to the boil slowly, simmering gently for ten minutes.
Transfer the fish into a serving dish, reserving the milk. Cover and keep warm.
Melt the butter in a saucepan, add the flour and cook gently for 2 minutes, then gradually add the milk, bring to the boil then simmer for 2 minutes stirring constantly until thick and smooth.
Stir in the hard-boiled eggs.
Put the two uncooked eggs on the top of the haddock, gently pour over the sauce and place in the oven for 4 minutes until set, sprinkle with chopped parsley and serve with oatcakes

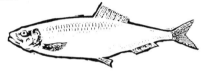

HERRINGS EDWARD VII
(Frank & Mary Kitts,
The Red Lion, Burscough)

Two friends of mine who have been in the catering trade for quite a number of years tell me this was of the favourite dishes of King Edward VII.

Buy boneless herring fillets, toss them well in flour, egg-wash & coarse oatmeal until they are well coated.
The fry them until they are golden brown in hot dripping for about 6 minutes and serve on warm muffins.

KIDNEYS ON TOAST
(Lorraine & Steven, Wigan)

Kidney's have been a favourite breakfast dish since Victorian times, a popular dish in the Wigan area even today.

This recipe originates from the Colne area and came from a 19th century recipe book.

Skin, halve and skewer the kidneys until they are flat. Season them well with salt, pepper and cayenne pepper.
Mix a quarter of a teaspoon of grated lemon rind and a little salt and pepper with a beaten egg, dip the kidneys in this mixture and then into fresh breadcrumbs. Fry them quickly in butter. Serve them on ovals of buttered toast with a full breakfast.

BARLICK KIPPERED CREAMS (1900)
Sam Richardson

Barnoldswick is a beautiful area near to Colne & Nelson and home of some of the finest hostelries in the North. This recipe comes from a grand old lady who remembers having kippered creams cooked for her by her grandmother in the late 1900s.

Buy boneless kipper fillets, then rub them through a wire sieve into a basin. Add the yolks of two eggs, the white of one egg, and season well with salt and fresh ground black pepper, and two tablespoons of thick cream. Put the mixture into little moulds or little cake cases, and bake them until their tops are nice and brown.
Serve with home-made warm bread.

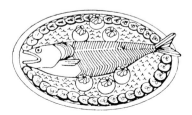

GAME PIE FOR A HUNTING BREAKFAST 1861
(Suzanne & Martyn Cahill)

This one pie would have kept a family of six for 3 weeks in food, for breakfast, dinner and tea. Whatever was left from this dish was served to the servants in the big houses. This was very popular in the Inn's of the north served with good ale.

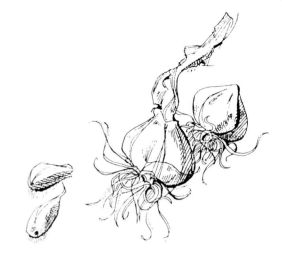

You would need one goose, one turkey, one snipe, two grouse, two woodcocks, one pheasant, two partridges, one bullocks tongue, the meat of one hare, one pint of good gravy, one pound of grated ham, seven pounds of flour, one and a quarter pounds of suet, and two pounds of butter.
Make an ornamental crust with the flour, suet and butter, in a fancy shape, with a top to fit, and bake in a slow oven. cut all the game and bullock's tongue into small pieces(

removing all the fat and bones) and stew them gently for two hours. Put it into the crust, adding the gravy and grated cooked ham, and a little seasoning if required. Cover with paste top, and warm in a slow oven.

This game pie would have cost in 1800 three shillings and ninepence today it would cost around £230.00, costing about £10.00 per portion.

BREAKFAST AND THE POOR HOUSEHOLD

Breakfast for the poor was something which I have experienced by trying all the food mentioned and it is not food I would like to have had every month, never mind every day.

In the cramped and spartan conditions of the homes of the poor of the north were no luxuries such as carpets, armchairs and beds. There was only an open fire with a home-made spit and a rude table and bench for the head of the family to sit at. The bed was a sack of straw, spread out in the same room that they ate in.

The smell in these tiny houses must have been terrible. During the early years of the 19th century outbreaks of Asiatic cholera, commonly designated cholera morbus or 'Black Fever', caused many deaths throughout England; tar barrels were burnt in the public streets to disinfect the atmosphere.

In *A Chronological History of Bolton*, 1800 James Clegg wrote: 'Distress of the Handloom Weavers':

> The weavers were labouring under the most incredible privation, they did not earn a sufficiency to procure them meat, except occasionally, more frequently once a week. Their ordinary food was oatmeal and potatoes, mutton broth, gruel, mutton dripping on stale bread, water and beer. A man having a family of five children could not with the assistance of his wife and two of his children earn more the two & three quarter pennies for each per day, applicable for food and clothing. There were 10,000 poor persons living upon 'twopence a day' in Bolton.
> The poor would queue for penny pieces of bacon of which, as a girl who had purchased a penny worth commented there is little here for six of us.'
> Another family of 12 ate only gruel twice a day, potatoes once and herrings sometimes. The pan they used was borrowed and their clothes were Pawned at night to redeem their bedding and their bedding in the morning to redeem their clothes.

Here are the two breakfast recipes these families lived on three twice a day, four days a week if they were lucky.

GRUEL

Two tablespoonful of oatmeal, half a blade of mace, three quarters of a pint of water.
Mix two spoonfuls of oatmeal very smooth in a little water, and gradually to three quarters of a pint of water, add half a blade of mace, set it over the fire for a quarter of an hour, stirring it constantly, add sugar to taste. (If you could afford it).

MUTTON BROTH

Three pounds of scrag of mutton, three quarts of water, two turnips, one tablespoon of pearl barley or rice.

Boil in three quarts of water, three pounds of scrag end of neck, with two turnips sliced, and a tablespoon of pearl barley or rice.
Let it boil for three hours, keeping it well skimmed.

RECIPES FOR THE POOR
(Warnes Model Cookery 1868)

This is a collection of recipes from one of my favourite antique cookery books, which shows you how the poor would have eaten

SUNDAY DINNER FOR SEVEN PERSONS

Take one pound of bacon and one pound of leg of beef. Put these into the pot without any water, and cook two hours, according to directions before given.
Five ounces of meat and a pint of nutritious gravy will be saved by this process, as compared with the ordinary method of boiling

A GALLON OF SOUP

Clean a sheep's head well, cut it in halves, put it into the pot, sprinkle with pepper and salt, add four onions (sliced), two small turnips, one carrot, a sprig of thyme and some parsley.
Water, three pints. and cook.

A DINNER FOR NINE PERSONS

Cut up two rabbits, add pepper and salt and a few herbs, .put same into a pot with one pint of water. Cover all with suet-pudding three inches thick. Cook for two hours.

THE BACON DINNER OF ENGLAND FOR EIGHT PERSONS

Put two pounds of bacon into the pot, without water. Cook for two and a half hours, when it will be four ounces heavier than if it had been cooked in water.

BRAWN
(Elizabeth Raffald, 1769)

Brawn was sold at all market area's in the North West, but do you know how it was made!

Get a small pig's head, and after seeing that it has been properly cleaned, put it into a pan with a pound and a half of lean beef, and enough cold water to cover it.
Bring gradually to the boil, and just before it boils, skim the water. Boil for two to three hours, until the meat comes easily from the bones, then put the meat into a hot pan, with the beef, chopping it up as quickly as you can. Sprinkle with a mixture of two tablespoonfuls of salt, two teaspoonfuls of pepper, a little cayenne and six cloves pounded up. Stir well together, and put into cake-tins, keeping it well pressed down for some hours, until the brawn is quite cold. To remove, dip the tin into hot water, and the brawn will slide out.

The liquor from the meat was used for pea soup and the dripping on bread, or for frying.

HODGE PODGE 1850

Take a pound of beef, a pound of veal and a pound of scrag of mutton.

Cut the beef into small pieces and put the whole into a saucepan, with two quarts of water. Take an ounce of barley, an onion, a small bundle of sweet-herbs, three or four heads of celery washed clean and cut small, a little mace, two or three cloves and some whole pepper tied all in a piece of cloth, and throw into the pot with the meat, three turnips pared and cut into two, a large carrot scraped clean and cut into six pieces and a small lettuce.

Cover the pot close and let it stew very gently for five or six hours; then take out the spice, sweet herbs and onion, pour all into a soup dish, season it with salt and send it to the table.

Hodge Podge is very similar to Lancashire Hot Pot. Taken from Warnes cookery book 1868 the recipe for 'Hotch Potch' is one pint of peas, 3lb lean end of a loin of mutton, 1 gal water, 4 carrots, 4 turnips, 1 onion, 1 head of celery, salt and pepper to taste. If you take the 'ch' off the end you have Hot Pot, there must be a connection.

Sheeps' trotters were made into a dish in the fourteenth century with eggs, pepper, salt, saffron and raisins. Collared pork is made from the gelatinous parts of the pig, as the ears, feet and face, and was in use from the first cookery book in 1300 according to the following recipe:-

GELE of FLESSH
(Forme of Cury A.D. 1390)

'Take swyn' fet and snowt' and the eerys, capons' conyin'g caln' fete, and waische he clene, and do he to seethe in the thriddel of wyne and vyneg' and wat and make forth as bifore.

CALFS FEET
(The Frugal Housewife, Manchester, 1811)

Parboil them then take out the long bones, split them and put them into a stew pan with some veal gravy and a glass of white wine. Add likewise the yolks of two or three eggs beat up with a little butter. Stir it till it is of a good thickness; and when the whole has gently simmered for about ten minutes, put the feet into your dish, and pour the sauce over them. Garnish with sliced lemon.

PIGEONS in SAVOURY JELLY
Mrs Elizabeth Raffald 1789

Roast your pigeons with the head and feet on, put a sprig of myrtle in their bills, make a jelly for them , pour a little into a bason, when it is set lay in the pigeons with their breast down, fill up your bowl with jelly, and turn it out.

25

Chapter 3

FAVOURITE NORTHERN FARE

The memories of my childhood are so clear, when I think of the week-ends. The smell of freshly baked bread, Eccles cakes and my mother's tatie pie. My dad used to make a stew that you could stand a fork up in, he never did give me the name of that recipe except that when he was out in Puna, or was it Bengal, or it could have been Egypt, that this mass of vegetables, meat and the Bisto twins were blended together and produced for the entire King's Regiment.

And this would not be a true northern recipe book without those wonderful week-end lunches which included my mother's Tatie Pie which nobody could repeat. My mother is just like yours — the BEST IN THE WORLD — and I wouldn't swap her for a gold clock (and my dad of course). The one ingredient that gives this recipe its unique flavour is the black pudding around the top before the suet crust.

And my mum always cooks the dish before she adds the black pudding and puts on her full of flavour suet pastry.

Dedicated to my dad NOBBY from the woman in your life, my lovely mum.

TATIE PIE
(Bolton, 1958)

675g (1 1/2lb) Rough Mince Beef
450g (1lb) peeled and cubed potatoes
2 medium onions, roughly chopped
2 large carrots, peeled and cubed
2 beef Oxo cubes
3 tablespoons of ahhhhhh Bisto
1 litre of water
1 whole bury black pudding
(skinned and sliced)
Salt
Fresh ground black pepper

Mothers recipe for Pastry

2 cups of plain flour
1 cup of shredded suet
pinch of salt
pinch of ground black pepper
125g (4 oz) best butter
3 to 4 tablespoons of cold water
1 egg yolk

Method for pastry

Sift the flour into a mixing bowl, add the suet, salt & pepper.

Blend in the butter lightly with your fingertips. When the mixture if fine, add the egg yolk and water binding into a stiff dough. Knead lightly for 5 minutes. Roll to cover the dish you are using for the Tatie Pie.

 ## TATIE PIE

My mother uses my late grandmother's brown earthenware 3-pint dish for her pie.

Make up the stock cubes with the litre of boiling water. Add the mince meat and vegetables to the casserole pour over the stock. Cook covered for one half hours at Gas 4,350F Don't forget to season.

Remove from the oven then add the Bisto made into a paste with cold water, blend this in well, top with slices of black pudding and finish off with the pastry. Egg wash the top, place back into the oven for 30 minutes or until the crust is golden brown.

Serve with red cabbage and a pint of traditional beer.

POOR MAN'S GOOSE
(Dorothy & Walter,
The Windmill, Parbold)
The best bar meals in Parbold

A very cheap meal as the name suggests, this recipe was popular all over England not just in the north during the years of rationing. When the rent man came a-knocking and there was no money left to feed the meter to light the gas mantle, this was the grub they lived on.

Any left-overs you can find (leave the cat alone) — i.e. cold meats, bacon, cooked vegetables ect — are blended with 4 eggs, half pint of fresh milk, 125g of stale or any cheese, grated.

Season with fresh ground black pepper & salt. Cut all the left overs into small pieces, mix well together and place in a well greased pie dish. Sprinkle with a little more cheese and cook slowly at Gas 3, 325F for 1 hour.

Alternatively use my mother's pastry recipe on page (000) and top with suet crust pastry

Years ago Pan Pie was a favourite Rochdale dinner time dish, it was served straight from the pan in which it had been cooked, topped with a suet lid.

It was on the evening of Saturday 21st December 1844, that a little shop, owned in common by 28 working men of Rochdale who called themselves the 'Pioneers' each having subscribed £1.00 opened its doors. The rent of the shop was £10 per annum. When the shop opened its stock consisted of 50lb butter, 56lb of sugar, 6cwt. of flour, one cwt. of oatmeal and two dozen candles.

The shop assistant was one of the twenty eight men who took turns, two evenings a week, serving the other pioneers. What was this business? — the Co-operative Society or as we know it the CO-OP.

PAN PIE
(Rochdale 1878)

*Dedicated to Sir Cyril Smith. M.P. for whom I
have cooked many a Lancashire meal.*

450g (1lb) Stewing Steak cubed
125g (4 ozs) diced kidney
1 large onion, peeled and sliced
1 large carrot, peeled & sliced
1 small turnip, peeled & diced
1 ltr of good beef stock
salt & pepper
suet pastry lid (see page 26)

Place all the ingredients, except the suet
pastry lid into a large pan. Simmer slowly for
two hours, add sliced potatoes until the pan
is full, seasoning well, cook for a further half
hour, topping up with stock if needed.

Top the pan with the suet pastry, making a
small hole in the pastry. Cook for a further
three quarters of an hour and serve from the
pan.

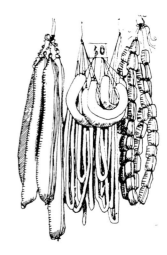

MORECAMBE BAY POTTED SHRIMPS
(Matty, Tish & Steven O'Neil)

This is great for a light snack, other
shrimps may be used for potting, but the
brown one from Morecambe Bay are the
best. The butter which is used to seal the
prawns should be used for spreading on
the brown bread which should be served
with this dish.

275ml (half pint) picked shrimps
75g (3 oz) best butter
pinch of grated nutmeg & mace salt
7 pepper to taste

Place all the ingredients into a saucepan and
heat them slowly, stirring very carefully until
the shrimps are well coated with butter. Do
not overheat. Place in small ramekins and
cover with the melted butter. Serve with
brown bread and thinly sliced lemon pieces.

TRIPE

There used to be hundreds of tripe dressers in the North, but it is sad to see that there are very few left.

For those who do not know about tripe, I am here to assure you that tripe is cooked in the cleansing process.

The two popular types of tripe eaten in the north are White tripe with the honeycomb look is used for Tripe & Onions and Black Tripe, which is used in a great deal of restaurants where they would egg-wash the tripe, breadcrumbs, then deep fry it, served with a warm onion sauce it is a great delicacy and favourite of the northern folk.

My father likes his served cold with salt, pepper and a dash of malt vinegar. I myself like it stuffed with slices of black pudding, topped with bacon and served with mushy peas, my mother cooks hers in milk with onions and cubed potatoes.

There are several recipes but I am sure you would like this one.

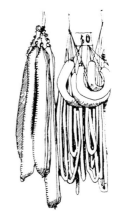

TRIPE STUFFED WITH BLACK PUDDING
(authors recipe)

675g (1.1/2 lb.) Dark tripe
1 Black Pudding, skinned and finely chopped
1 large onion thinly sliced
1 tablespoon of English Mustard
salt & pepper
12 rashers of streaky bacon
12 wooden cocktail sticks

Cut the tripe into 3 X 6 inch strips (15x8 cm), you should get 6 pieces from one & half pound, with bits left, which you should chop very fine and put to one side. Spread a thinlayer of mustard on each strip of tripe, sprinkle with black pudding and the bits of tripe, season.

Roll them tightly , wrap with two rashers of streaky bacon, holding together by piercing through the mid centre with wooden cocktail sticks. Place them in a tray greased with a little dripping. Bake for in the oven for 1 hour at 180C, 350f, gas 4.

WORDSWORTH'S BACON AND APPLE HOT POT
(Colin Cooper English)

This Cumbrian recipe, which was once part of the Lancashire boundary is said to be Wordsworth's Lancashire Lakeland recipe.

Wordsworth was a Cumbrian, but he celebrated his schooldays and youth in Lancashire, drew his first poetic inspiration from it, described it in his first stanzas, and packed his autobiography with Lancashire scenes and episodes.

The meeting-place of the poets and essayists was in Lancashire at Storrs Hall.

1.4 kg (3 lb) boiling bacon, trimmed
and cubed
450g (1lb) Granny Smiths,
peeled, cored and thinly sliced
2 large onion sliced
4 small carrots sliced
1 turnip sliced
2 tablespoons of black treacle
4 large potatoes sliced
a pinch of mace, sage & thyme
Pepper to taste

Soak the bacon in cold water for 5 hours.

Drain and put into a large saucepan with the vegetables, apple & herbs cover with a little stock or cold water.

Bring to the boil and simmer for one & half hours.

This was usually served with boiled cabbage and brown bread.

LOBSCOUSE
(C.J.Fitzpatrick, Bootle)

I grew up with several Liverpudlians, Eric Royal, Teddy Burke & big Alan Metcalfe who talked fondly of the food they were brought up on. Without exception this is the most popular food from the people of Liverpool. The recipe, put together from my father-in-law who was born in Liverpool & now lives in the area of Bootle which was once part of the Lancashire boundary

675g (1-2lb) Silverside of beef,
soaked overnight, cut into cubes
50g (2oz) dripping
3 large onions, sliced
1.4kg (3lb) potatoes, sliced
2 carrots sliced
225g (8 oz) dried peas, soaked overnight
1 ltr of good beef stock
seasoning

Melt the dripping in a deep casserole, seal of the beef. Drain the peas and lob all the ingredients into the casserole. Pour on the stock adding enough water if necessary cover with the peas, place on a laid and cook at Gas 2, 300f, 150c for 3 to 4 hours.

CORNED BEEF HASH
(Robert White)

Easy and simple to make, every northern granny will give you the same recipe, for which I have recipes dating back has far as 1846.

450g (1lb) tin of corned beef
1 large onion chopped finely
1 pint of beef stock (thickened
with cornflour)
1 tablespoon mushroom ketchup
900g (2lb) cooked and mashed potatoes
(seasoned and butter added)
50g (2 ozs) grated cheddar cheese
50g (2 ozs) butter
Freshly ground black pepper

Chop the cooked corned beef into half inch cubes, place into a deep dish, topped with onion, sprinkle with mushroom ketchup, pour on the beef stock. Top with mashed potato, the melted butter and grated cheese. Place in a medium oven Gas 4, 350f, 180c for 20 minutes until golden brown.
(Young Thomas will cook this when he gets older).

MORECAMBE BAY PRAWNS IN JACKET POTATO
(Andy Britton)

I spent a great deal of time in the Ribchester area creating new recipe's for a large food company and training chefs in several hotels in the Lancashire area. One of the recipes I learned was this one from the White Bull several years ago.

100g (4 oz) peeled cooked prawns
30ml (2 tbsp) white wine
50g (2 oz) best butter (melted)
50g (2 oz) plain sifted flour
225ml (8 fl oz) fresh milk with cream
100ml (4 fl oz) fresh Orange Juice
Freshly Ground Black Pepper
Zest and Juice of 1 lemon
salt
4 cooked Jacket Potatoes
1 sprig of fresh parsley

Put the butter, flour, milk & orange into a saucepan. Heat, whisking continuously, until the sauce thickens and is very smooth.

Simmer for 2 minutes seasoning well with salt & ground black pepper, add the white wine, prawns & lemon juice. Cook for a further 2 minutes.

Open the jacket potatoes and top with the Whitby prawns in sauce.

COLNE BACON & EGG FLAN
(Barrowford 1907)

Travelling around Colne, I have made some very good friends.

I also was taught the art of the perfect Yorkshire Pudding, which will follow this recipe.

175g (6 oz) short crust pastry (see page 26)
175g (6 oz) rindless lean green bacon rashers
50g (2 oz) grated cheese
3 eggs
150ml (1/4 pint) single cream
1 sprig of parsley finely chopped
salt and pepper

Pre-heat the oven to Gas 5, 375F, 190c.
Roll the pastry large enough to line a 18cm (7 inch) fluted flan case. Chop the bacon very fine, whisk the eggs with the cream and season well. Pour the mixture into the flan case, sprinkle with bacon & grated cheese.

Bake the flan in the centre of the oven for 30 minutes until set and golden brown.

YORKSHIRE PUDDING —
The Lancashire Way

For Jack Hampson, who for the last 30 years tries to cook!

I have one of the finest collections of antique cookery books with over 45 different ways to make Yorkshire Pudding. In my Elizabeth Raffald 1794, she describes it A Yorkshire Pudding to bake under meat, using four eggs. William Kitchiner uses 3 eggs in The *Cooks Oracle*, 1827 and also says The true Yorkshire Pudding is about half an inch thick when done; but it is the fashion in London to make them full twice that thickness". To insult the Yorkshire Pudding, I feel is a disgrace and that is exactly what Charles Elme Francatelli did in his *Cooks Guide* of 1869. This so called chef who copied everybody's work always had to add to other people's recipes. Chief cook to H.M. Queen Victoria, he added nutmeg to his recipe.

I suspect that the *Larousse Gastronomique*,(the worlds greatest cookery reference book) must have taken their recipe from Francatelli also, has they are the only two books I have read that uses nutmeg in Yorkshire Pudding.

But it was Hannah Glasse in 1747, who gave the name and described it in her *Art of Cookery* "It is an excellent good pudding; the gravy of the meat eats well with it".

THE PERFECT YORKSHIRE PUDDING
By the Author
Dedicated to the Newburgh PTA
& Newburgh School

30ml (2 tbsp) beef dripping
100g (4 oz) Plain flour (sifted)
a pinch of salt
1 fresh (large) egg
200ml (7 fl oz) fresh milk
100ml (3 fl oz) water

Pre-heat the oven to gas 7, 425f, 220c
Into a clean bowl, mix the flour and a pinch of salt, make a well in the centre and break in the egg. Add half the milk, using a wooden spoon, work in the flour slowly. Beat the mixture until it is smooth, then add the remaining milk and the 100ml of water.

Beat until it is well mixed.

Put the dripping from the beef into a large baking tin or individual yorkshire pudding tray until the fat is very hot (smoking). Pour the batter and return to the oven to cook for 35-40 minutes, until risen and golden brown. DO NOT OPEN THE DOOR AT ALL FOR AT LEAST 30 MINUTES.

TOAD IN'TH HOLE
(for Dr Richard Underwood, Parbold)

Another one of those northern recipes that you hear the old wives' tales about. Over two hundred years ago was told the fairy tale of Diamonds or Toads? — which is it to be, girls, diamonds or toads! — in which the good girl is endowed with the faculty of scattering diamonds and pearls around her, while the unsatisfactory girl is condemned to distribute toads in the same fashion. Now, which will you choose? Why make a choice, some matter of fact little maiden remarks, for fairy stories are not true. The word in this issue is cheapness (toad).

The hole is the dish in which the cheap meat is used. Mrs Beeton used rump steak and sheeps kidney in her recipe in 1861.

Queen Victoria's chef Francatelli copied her recipe and in 1868 Mary Jewry wrote for her recipe take 1 chicken & veal.

Yet my grandmother's recipe is sausage. In a modern cookery book I have read 'Toad in the Hole' use chuck steak', It is too obvious that this was a poor person's meal. And here are the three versions which I have modernised for you.

Mrs Beeton (1861)

450g (1lb) Rump Steak
1 sheep's kidney diced
seasoning
300ml (10 floz) Yorkshire Pudding
mixture (page 000)

Fry the diced steak & kidney for 10 minutes in good dripping and season well. Place them into a roasting tray and into a pre- heated oven at 425f (mark 7) , for a further ten minutes. Remove the tin from the oven. Pour over the batter and cook for a further 30 minutes, until the batter is well-risen.

Mary Jewry (1868)

A chicken, some veal stuffing, 3 eggs, 1 pint of milk, some flour

Draw, bone and truss a chicken, fill it with veal stuffing.

Making a batter with a pint of milk, 3 eggs and sufficient flour to make it thick, pour it deep into buttered dish. Place the fowl in the centre of the batter, and bake in the oven as above.

Use 450g (1lb) Chicken meat diced and 100g (4 ozs diced Veal for the modern version.

Jessie Tong
(author's grandmother)

This is the more well known method for a lot of people in the north.

450g (1lb) Thornley's Pork or
Cumberland Sausage
600g (20 fl oz) Yorkshire pudding
batter (page 32)

Grease a roasting tin with a tablespoon of dripping, and place the sausages into it. Place the tin in a pre-heated oven at Gas 7 425F for 12 minutes. Remove the tin from the oven, and pour over the batter. Return to the oven for 30 -35 minutes.

Serve with Bubble & Squeak.

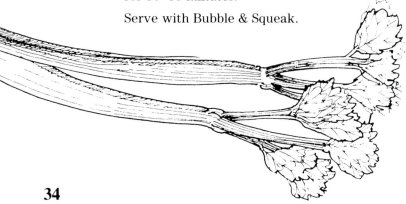

BUBBLE & SQUEAK

Bubble and squeak, a fry up, was a favourite during the eighteenth century, nineteenth century and today's twentieth century. The earliest use of the term so far discovered was in *A Burlesque Translation of Homer* written by my namesake Thomas Bridges in 1767.

'We therefore cook'd him up a dish of lean bull-beef with cabbage fried and a full pot of beer beside: Bubble they call this dish, and squeak; Our taylors dine on't thrice a week'.

Potatoes and Cabbage fried with beef pieces, fried separately was the next form at the beginning of the 19th century.

Dr Kitchiner's Recipe, 1823 'When 'midst the frying Pan, in accents savage, The Beef, so surly, quarrels with the cabbage.' Here he used slices of rather underdone cold boiled salted beef; butter; a cabbage; pepper and salt.

For more on the life of William Kitchiner MD and his famous cookery book the Cooks Oracle do read *A Regency Eccebtric* by Tom Bridge & Colin Cooper English, published by Southover Press.

Mrs Marie Rundle in 1846 to Boil, chop and fry with a little butter, pepper and salt, some cabbage and lay on it slices of underdone beef, lightly fried.

Francatelli in his five shilling Cooks Guide of 1869 told us:

> This is a favourite dish with some people, and is available when it happens that you have had boiled beef the day before; it is certainly preferable to a cold dinner.
>
> Cut the beef and its fat in slices about the sixth of an inch thickness, and fry them quickly over a brisk fire, just enough to warm the meat through without drying it, and dish it up round some chopped or small cut dressed cabbage, carrots and parsnips, seasoned with pepper and salt, and fried with butter. No sauce.
>
> Note:- It is usual when people fond of bubble-and-squeak to boil sufficient vegetables with the beef for a dish of bubble-and-squeak the next day.

Today we fry it up with chopped onion, mashed potato and cabbage.

> We need a pan that's lined with grease
> to put the cabbage chopped,
> Then line with onions and mash spuds
> and mix together the lot.
>
> When frying lightly on the stove
> To this thy seasoning add,
> And with this dish,
> You serve good beef,
> And Bubble and Squeak you've had.

Author in 1983.

The north of England has some of the greatest resort areas, like Blackpool, with 17 million holiday visitors a year and Liverpool's Albert Dock with 29 million visitors. Merseyside, its culture and architecture, port and sport, commerce and industry are world famous. The outgoing nature is reflected in the welcome extended to everyone, whether you be a visitor or a resident of the City of Liverpool. The River Mersey and the breathtaking view of the waterfront. The architectural gems include Speke Hall, soap baron Lord Leverhulme's model village at Port Sunlight and Liverpool's two cathedrals. The Beatles draw many thousands of tourists and the Maritime Museum is a must for the seafarers of England to visit.

Southport is lively all year round. It is a golfer's dream with Royal Birkdale, Hesketh, Hillside, Southport and Ainsdale, Formby and West Lancashire. With the Flower Show in full bloom every August. One recipe I have had given to me comes from Executive Chef of The Royal Clifton Hotel in Southport, Mr Chris Pleasant.

Chris tells me this can be eaten hot or cold and was usually served for lunch with beer in the old Inns of the North.

SPICED BEEF IN RED WINE
(The Royal Clifton Hotel, Southport.)

1.15kg (2.1/2 lb) of Sirloin or Brisket
450ml (16 fl oz) red wine
Half teaspoon of the following
salt,
pepper,
marjoram,
winter savoury,
ground mace,
nutmeg and thyme
1 large bunch of parsley finely chopped
1 egg yolk

Place the beef into a very large and deep saucepan, covering it with water, bring it to the boil, reduce the heat and leave it to simmer for 1 hour.

Mix together all the herbs, parsley and spices, blending them into a paste with the egg yolk.

Remove the beef and allow it to cool in a deep baking tray.

Make deep slits with a sharp knife into the beef towards the centre of the beef, filling the slits with the herb mixture.

Pour over the wine and bake in a moderate oven gas mark 2, 300f 150C for 2 hours.

Serve with a selection of fresh vegetables.

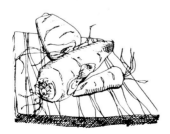

HINDLE WAKES

"Old hens were sold at the wakes" (fairs) which gave this dish Hen de la Wake its name, originally from Bolton-le-Moors. If you have ever had this recipe without the prunes, then it was not Hindle Wakes.

1 x 1.4kg/ 3 lb boiling fowl
450g/ 1lb Prunes
6 pieces of rindless streaky bacon
2 lemons
50g/ 2 ozs breadcrumbs
1 small onion, finely chopped
1 pinch of thyme
1 pinch of basil salt
freshly milled pepper
rich brown gravy

Wash the lemon and pare the rind thinly and simmer it gently for 15 minutes to extract the flavour. Add to this the strained juice of the lemons.

Wash the prunes and pour the lemon juice over them, letting them soak overnight.

Stone the prunes, blend them with the onion, thyme, basil and breadcrumbs, seasoning well and stuffing the chicken with the mixture.

Steam the chicken for 4 hours. Then wrap the chicken in bacon and roast in a pre-heated oven at Gas 4 180c (350f) for 35 minutes.

Serve with a rich gravy garnished with prunes.

LAMBS LIVER, BACON & ONION
(Phil Taylor of Booker-Fitch)

450g/1lb lambs liver, cut into strips
2 large onions, thinly sliced
225g/8 ozs streaky bacon, rindless, (grilled)
100g/4 ozs button mushrooms
300ml/half pint of beef stock
30ml/2 tablespoons Worcestershire sauce
15ml/1 tablespoon plain flour
salt
freshly mill pepper
30g/1 oz good dripping

Melt the dripping in a large frying pan and gently fry the sliced onions for 4 minutes until transparent. Coat the liver strips with the flour and add to the pan with the mushrooms. Fry for a further 4 minutes, stirring well, then add the beef stock, bring to the boil, add the Worcestershire sauce and chopped slices of bacon, season and serve with mashed potatoes.

From Florence Whites *'Good Things In England'* 1929.

An Excellent Lancashire Hot-Pot

Manchester is noted for its hot-pots and has a special one of its own but the following excellent recipe hails from Bolton-le-Moors. The oysters may be omitted, but they are the correct thing in a real hot pot.

Another correct thing is to serve Lancashire hot-pot with a dish or glass jar of pickled red cabbage whatever recipe be used. This is traditional.

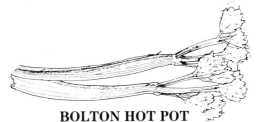

BOLTON HOT POT
(converted by Author)

900g/2lb Middle neck of mutton, trimmed, cut into chops
900g/2 lb thinly sliced potatoes
30g/1 oz good dripping
1 large onion
5ml/1 pint of beef stock
30g/1 oz plain flour
salt
freshly milled pepper
225g/8 oz button mushrooms
4 Lambs kidneys, core removed, cut fine
10 oysters, washed and beard removed

Melt the dripping in a large frying pan, brown off the chops.

Remove and place them into a large earthenware casserole with lid. Cook the onions, add the flour and cook for a minute, add the stock, season, remove from the heat, stirring to make a nice smooth gravy.

Put the kidneys, mushrooms, oysters with the chops, interlay the potatoes with all the ingredients. Pour over the gravy and cook in a moderate oven Gas Mark 5 190c (375f) for 2 hours. Take off the lid during the last 15 minutes to brown the potatoes nicely.

LOVE IN DISGUISE
An 18th Century Jest

The amount of work that went into this heart, show that northerners, do have a love of cookery and not just eating.

1 calf's heart
bread-crumbs 4 oz
finely chopped suet 2 tablespoonfuls
parsley chopped fine 2 teaspoonfuls
sweet marjoram 1 teaspoonful
lemon the grated rind of half
minced ham 2 oz
pepper quarter teaspoonful
salt half teaspoonful
made mustard half teaspoonful
egg 1
vermicelle 1 oz
four or five slices of fat bacon
a piece of greaseproof paper
gravy flavoured with tomato, and rather redish colour

TIME: 2 hours

Break up the vermicelli into short lengths and simmer it in boiling stock for 10 to 15 minutes, lift out, drain, and let it go cold.

Remove all the pipes from the inside of the heart, clean it well, and let it lie in cold water for an hour.

Make the stuffing with the breadcrumbs, suet, parsley, sweet marjoram, grated lemon rind, mince ham, pepper, salt, made mustard, egg.

Wipe the heart dry, stuff it, wrap the rashers of fat bacon over it so that it keeps the stuffing in; skewer them on with small skewers.

Wrap the whole heart in greaseproof paper, spread thick with dripping, tie round and put into a baking tin.

Bake in a good oven for one and half hours, take out; remove the paper; brush all over with yolk of egg and roll in coarse bread-crumbs mixed with cooked vermicelli which should be in quite short lengths to represent prickles.

Return to oven and cook for another half hour until nicely browned. Dish up and serve with a good brown or tomato gravy.

This dish was recently done by my mother for my father, who loves heart.

SHEEP'S TROTTERS

A Bolton lady wrote: 'We eat sheep's trotters boiled in Bolton. It is a sort of ritual. When the Football Wanderers bring home the Cup, they are received with sheep's trotters decorated with white and blue ribbons.'

Recipe (1830)

Sheeps trotters;
stock;
sweet herbs;
a little flour,
milk;
pepper and salt;
yolks of 1 or 2 eggs;
some verjuice (crab apple juice)
or lemon juice

Wash the feet well, changing the water repeatedly. Put into some old stock with a bunch of sweet herbs. Boil up until the bones can be easily taken out. Lift out herbs and return the meat to the saucepan.

Thicken the stock with flour, mixed with milk. Season with pepper and salt. Stir in the yolks of one or two eggs according to richness required, and sharpen with verjuice.

n.b. These recipes would most certainly be lost if not written down. I wonder if the Lion of Vienna, Nat Lofthouse was ever presented with sheeps feet.

PORCUPINE
of the FLAT RIBS of BEEF
(Mrs Raffald 1770)

Bone the flat ribs, and beat it half an hour with a paste-pin (rolling pin), then rub it over with the yolks of eggs, strew over it breadcrumbs, parsley, leeks, sweet-marjoram, lemon-peel shred fine, nutmeg, pepper, and salt, roll it up very close, and bind it hard, lard it across with bacon, then a row of cold boiled tongue, a third row of pickled cucumbers, a fourth row of lemon-peel: do it over in rows as above till it is larded all round, it will look like red, green, white, and yellow dices, then split it and put it in a deep pot with a pint of water, lay over a caul of veal, to keep it from scorching, tie it down with strong paper, and send it to the oven; when it comes out skim off the fat, and strain your gravy (stock) into a sauce-pan, add to it two spoonfuls of red wine, the same of browning, one of mushroom catchup, half a lemon, thicken it with a lump of butter rolled in flour, dish up the meat, and pour the gravy on the dish, lay round forcemeat-balls; garnish with horse-radish, and serve it up.

N.B. In the north 200 years ago we served beef with horseradish.

The Victorian Lancashire Lunch:

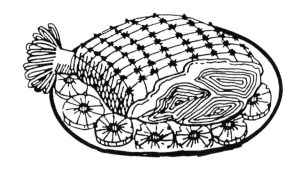

Most of the above recipes were served at "LUNCH" time. "LUNCH" is a modern abbreviation of 'luncheon' which in its original form "LUNCHIN" nothing but a big slice or lump of bread or other eatable. This would be particularly applicable to the big lump of bread or cheese off which the workers of the north still make their midday meal. In the north it is known as 'snap'.

Gay wrote in 1714, "I sliced the luncheon from the barley-loaf". The sense of the word was in course of time easily extended to that of the light meal we now eat at noon. Though the original sense of luncheon was a noonday slice or lump of bread or cheese.

It may be worthwhile mentioning here that the now familiar 'Sandwich' which is part of lunch, supper, picnics and outings, and the long distance lorry driver's best friend, gets its name from the fourth Earl of Sandwich who, being a confirmed gambler, invented it in order to remain at the gaming table without interruption (I don't think the saying, 'Put your money where your mouth is', came from the Earl).

Lunch was simple then as it is now, with chops, hashes, cold pork pies, cheese with raw onion (Ploughman's Lunch). The normal working family would live off cheese or herrings with rough bread, stout or water, if they could afford it. At twopence a day it was very expensive to have lunch.

TALKING A LOAD OF TRIPE

Tripe has had a remarkable history from the time the Roman Empire until its renewed prosperity under the UCP (United Cattle Products). The Romans set great store by it; Tripe was a delicacy that graced the feasts of nobles. All through English history from Chaucer, Lamb, Burns, Shakespeare to the great Charles Dickens. Tripe has received the meed of honourable praise from the chief wits and writers of England, having played an important part in the diet of democracy.

A food rich in nutriment and body-building qualities, the most digestible possible, food that is peculiarly suitable as a base for the most delicate of appetising dishes.

In the age of diets, fast food and food values. Tripe contains protein, fat, Creatinin, the basic substance of meat juice; Glycogen, animal starch; Sarolactic, a milk substance. This proves without doubt, tripe to be above all solid animal foods, one of the most body-building, nutritious, and easily digested of foods. It without doubt compares favourably with the rich man's oyster.

I asked David Hewitt, Marketing Manager at Thornley's Pork Butchers in Chorley, why there are very few shops now selling Tripe in the North West.

It is not in decline, but more in demand, the population of most Northern towns as doubled even tripled and we are selling more not less, when you mention tripe people turn their nose up at it because they do not know much about it. "I do believe you're going to put the question of talking aload of tripe to rights."

TRIPE A LA THORNLEY

500g/1lb Tripe, cut into small pieces
100g/4 oz Macaroni
4 large tomatoes, sliced
50g/2 oz grated cheese
25g/1 oz flour
25g/1 oz butter
600ml/1 pint fresh milk
300ml/half pint of seasoned vegetable stock
(hot)pinch of tarragon
salt
freshly milled pepper
freshly chopped parsley.

Place in a earthenware casserole the tripe, macaroni and sliced tomatoes, pour on the hot vegetable stock, cook on a medium heat for 20 minutes, stirring to prevent the macaroni from sticking. Add the milk, then add the butter and flour, stir until the sauce thickens and cook for a further 5 minutes, stirring continually. Top with tarragon and grated cheese, place under the grill for a few minutes, sprinkle with fresh parsley and serve.

STEWED TRIPE & ONIONS
(Graham Blakeway, Chorley)

500g/1lb Honeycomb Tripe,
cut into small pieces
2 large Onions, peeled and thinly sliced
25g/1 oz butter
25g/1 oz flour
600ml/1 pint of fresh milk
pinch nutmeg
salt
freshly milled pepper
4 slices of toast quartered and buttered

Into a large casserole place the chopped tripe and sliced onions,top with milk, sprinkle with nutmeg and 25g/1 oz butter. Cook in a pre-heated oven Gas 4, 180c/350f for 30 minutes. Add the sifted flour and seasoning, cook for further 5 minutes stirring all the time. Garnish with sippets of hot toast triangles.

'Jack Hampson's'
TRIPE & COWHEEL CASSEROLE

500g/1lb Tripe, roughly chopped
500g/1lb Cowheel, roughly chopped
(without bone)
2 onions, peeled, sliced
2 sticks of celery, sliced
2 carrots, peeled, sliced
2 large potatoes, peeled and diced
2 cloves
a sprig of thyme
600ml/1 pint of good beef stock
60ml/4 tablespoons port
25g/ 1 oz butter
25g/1 oz flour
salt
freshly milled pepper

Into a large casserole put the tripe, cowheel, vegetables, cloves, thyme, port and beef stock. Place in a pre-heated oven Gas 4, 180c/350f for 1 hour. Remove from the oven, add the butter and flour, season well, stirring until it thickens to a nice sauce consistency. Cook for a further 5 minutes and serve.

COWHEEL & TRIPE BRAWN
(Ted Reynolds, The Crown, Southport)

500g/1 lb Honeycombe Tripe, roughly cut
1 cowheel
500g/1lb lean Beef, roughly cut
salt
freshly milled pepper.

Into a large saucepan, place the tripe, cowheel and beef, easoning well with salt and pepper, cover with cold water and simmer for 5 hours. Skimming when necessary, being very careful the liquid does not reduce too much. Strain the stock into another clean saucepan. Remove the bones. Cut the meat, tripe and cowheel very small, return the meats then to the liquor. Season again very carefully, and pour into a mould or pattie tins to set.

POTTED TRIPE
(Pat Cobham)

225g/ 8 oz Tripe, finely minced
30ml/ 2 tablespoons cowheel stock
5ml/ 1 teaspoon tomato puree
1 pinch of nutmeg
1 pinch of mace
salt
freshly milled pepper
melted butter

Put the tripe through a mincing machine or blender with all the ingredients except the melted butter. Press into small pots, when set cover with a little melted butter. This really is excellent for sandwiches.

To Souse PIGS FEET and EARS
Mrs Raffald 1789

CLEAN Your pig's feet and ears, and boil them till they are tender, then split the feet, and put them into salt and water with the ears; when you use them dry well with a cloth, and dip them in batter made of flower and eggs, fry them good brown, and send them up with good melted butter.- N.B You may eat them cold; make fresh pickle every two days, and they will keep sometime.

To Souse TRIPE
Mrs Raffald 1789

WHEN your tripe is boiled, put it into salt and water, change the salt and water every day till you use it, dip it in batter,and fry it as the pigs feet and ears, or boil it in fresh salt and water, with an onion sliced, a few sprigs of parsley, and send melted butter for sauce.

Chapter 4

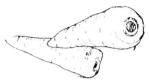

SOUPS

Soups are excellent for keeping the blood in a healthy alkaline condition as they are rich in organic mineral salts. Save all the outer leaves off vegetables to make a stock by boiling them and then straining off the liquid. This is a cheap medicine which can be flavoured with Marmite or Oxo and drank at bedtime. It gives full fitness in mind and body and is far healthier than tea or coffee. I have put together a collection of northern soups and broths that date as far back as 1727 to the 1950s. In honour of the Lancashire Borders I am opening this section with Lancashire Broth. The original recipe of 1763 I have converted, so you too can taste what it really was like to have soup before packets came into the SOUPerSTORES !..

LANCASHIRE BROTH
A Good and Substantial Dinner
for Five-pence per Head.

Wash ¾lb of scotch Barley in a little cold water, put it in a soup pot with a Shin or Leg of Beef, of about ten pounds weight, sawed into four pieces, (tell the butcher to do this for you,) cover it well with cold water, set it on the fire; when it boils skim it very clean, and put in two Onions of about three ounces weight each, set it by the side of the fire to simmer very gently about two hours; then skim all the fat clean off, and put in two heads of Celery, and a large Turnip cut into small squares; season it with salt, and let it boil an hour and a half longer; and it is ready: take out the meat (carefully with a slice, and cover it up and set it by the fire to keep warm): and scum the Broth well before you put it in the Tureen.

	s.	d.
Shin of Beef of 10lb	2	0
Three quarter pound of barley	0	4½
2 Onions of about 3 oz weight each	0	0½
Celery	0	1
Large Turnip	0	1
TOTAL	2	7

Thus you get four quarts of Good Soup, at 8d. per Quart.

Even in modern methods we have only knocked one hour of the time of three and half hours in 270 years. It is only the recipe of the last 150 years we have left the meat in.

LANCASHIRE BROTH
(Author revised recipe)

725g (1½lb) shin of beef, cubed
2 Pieces of Ox Tail
45ml (3 tablespoons) pearl barley
1 each of the following:
carrot, turnip & onion chopped
2 leeks, trimmed & chopped
salt & pepper

Put the meat into a saucepan cover with 2.3 litres (4 pints) water, season this well and bring slowly to the boil, covering and simmer for one hour and half.

Add the barley and chopped vegetables and simmer for a further hour, skimming off any fat and serve hot.

NETTLE SOUP
(Mary Whittle)

This soup is very good for you as the nettle is an excellent spring medicine for purifying the blood, being rich in sulphur, sodium and phosphates. It can be used as early spring kale is gathered when the tops are 6 to 8 inches high.

Gather some young nettle tops and wash them thoroughly, chopping them very finely and steam them in a little water. Add a pint of fresh , with milk a tablespoon of butter, seasoning, and thicken with flour or a little mashed potato.

TRADITIONAL TRIPE SOUP
(Chef, John Livingston)

When you see this recipe do not turn your nose up and think it sounds terrible because it tastes nothing like it sounds.

450g (1lb) Dressed Tripe
40 fl.ozs/2 pints water
1 turnip
1 carrot
2 small onions
Sweet herbs
Parsley
1 pint milk
3 tablespoons cornflour
salt & pepper
5 fl.oz/quarter pint of
fresh double cream

First scald the tripe and cut into very small pieces. Put in the herbs and one and half pints of cold water, bring to the boil.

Chop all the vegetables into small pieces, add the tripe and bring to the boil (simmering) for one hour. Add the cold milk and save a little to make a paste with the cornflour, add this to the soup, season and stir for 5 minutes. Add the cream and chopped parsley and serve.

45

BURY'S CURLEY GREEN SOUP
or FLAT-CAP SOUP
(Ann Merry, Newburgh Post Office)

This soup is what they called flat-cap soup. The old dears on the market day would go around collecting all the big green leaves from the curly cabbages and if it rained they would use them to cover their heads, hence flat-cap soup.

40 fl.oz/2 pints water
6 large leaves of green finely shredded
1 piece of grated turnip
1 tablespoon brown sago
(steeped in 1 cup of milk)
1 large onion finely chopped
1 tablespoon best butter
1 tablespoon Marmite

Put all the vegetables into cold water and bring to the boil.

Simmer for 2 hours then add the butter, Marmite, sago and seasoning which has been steeped in one cup of milk for an hour.

Stir well and allow to cook for 10 minutes before serving.

KIDNEY SOUP
(Cheryl Middleton, Farnworth)

450g/1lb Ox kidney
25g/1 oz butter
3 tablespoons plain flour
2 onions, peeled and chopped
1 small turnip, peeled and chopped
1 large carrot, peeled and chopped
1.2 ltr/2 pints beef stock (2 oxo cubes)
salt
freshly ground black pepper

Cut the kidney away from the core and chop into very small pieces. Season the flour, using half, toss the kidneys in to it.

Melt the butter in a large saucepan and fry the kidneys gently until lightly browned. Add the prepared vegetables, toss lightly and then add the stock. Bring to the boil, remove any scum that may rise, season well and simmer gently for 2 hours.

Blend the rest of the flour into a smooth paste with a little water, add some of the soup and mix them well together before returning to the soup. Simmer for a further 20 minutes and serve with fresh crusty bread.

CHICKEN BROTH
(Janet Kay 1926)

This must be one of the cheapest soups to make and no doubt one of the healthiest if you are elderly.

1 chicken carcass
1.2 ltr chicken stock (cubes)
25g/1 oz pearl barley
1 blade of mace
4 peppercorns
1 celery stalk, chopped
1 onion, peeled
salt.

Remove any chicken trimmings and flesh from the carcass and cut into small pieces. Break up the carcass with a large knife and put it into a large saucepan with the chicken stock and the rest of the ingredients.

Bring to the boil, reduce the heat and simmer for 2 hours. Strain through a fine sieve and replace into a clean saucepan, add the small pieces of chicken and re-heat.

LONGRIDGE LEEK AND POTATO SOUP
(Veronica Scott 1892)

6 leeks peeled and washed,
cut into thin slices
4 Large potatoes, diced and washed.
1 cup of rice
salt and pepper
1.2 ltr/2 pints of water
1 cup of breadcrumbs (brown & white)
1 tablespoon of cornflour blended
with 1 cup of milk.

Put the water into a large saucepan and bring to the boil, season well adding the potatoes and leeks. Add the rice after 15 minutes with the breadcrumbs, then simmer for a further hour. When cooked add the cornflour, thickened with a cup of milk. Dress with chopped parsley and a little double cream.

OYSTERS & ONION SOUP WITH PORT
(Owen Oyston, Blackpool F.C.)

I served this to a large dinner party, which I was asked to cook for by Owen Oyston, and it took no time at all to convert his flavour buds to the strains of Lancashire.

12 fresh oysters
450g/1lb onions, peeled and finely chopped
75g/3 oz leek, finely chopped
75g/3 oz best butter
750ml/1¼ pint chicken stock (stock cube)
200ml/7 fl.oz double cream
50ml/2 fl. oz fine ruby port
salt
freshly ground black pepper.

Wash and open the oysters. Reserve the juice, remove and reserve the beards.

Into a large saucepan place the butter and blanch the onions until they are transparent, add the leek, oyster juice and beards, chicken stock, salt and pepper. Simmer slowly for 30 minutes until all the ingredients are cooked. Pass the soup through a fine sieve. Put the soup into a clean saucepan and add the oysters, simmer for a further 5 minutes.

Stir in the cream and port and season to taste. Serve three oysters in each soup plate. Top with shredded leek.

THICK PEA SOUP WITH PIG'S TROTTERS
(Sue & Peter Vickers)

I can think of no better way to finish off the soup section than the 'stick to your ribs' Soup of Lancashire fame. A great deal of nineteenth century households kept a pig in the backyard, using household scraps and vegetable trimmings from the allotments to help feed it.

4 pigs trotters
110g/4 ozs dried peas
1.2 ltr/2 pints of water
1 large onion, finely chopped
1 small stick of celery, finely chopped
1 heaped teaspoon salt

Soak the peas overnight. Drain them well. Put all the ingredients into a large saucepan with a lid; bring slowly to the boil; simmering gently until the trotters are very tender. Very carefully lift out the trotters and remove the meat from the bones. Dice the meat and return it to the pan.

Serve with suet dumplings.

The following recipe will teach you several things. SPRINGWATER was used all those years ago, spinach, even today is used to give green colouring and the French definitely pinched fried bread (croutons) from the north of England.

Cornmeal Dumplings for Soups
1844 (modernised)

Mix a teacupful of corn meal with 2 ozs of plain flour, 1 oz suet, salt and pepper to taste, mix all together and make a dough with 4 tablespoons of water, shape into small balls, roll them in flour, and cook for 10 minutes in the boiling soup.

Potato Dumplings for Soups
1874 (modernised)

Boil 4 medium potatoes, mash them with a little butter and half beaten egg. Season with salt and pepper, then beat well in 2 ozs flour and 1 oz semolina. Add a little milk if it seems dry, but you are looking for a stiff paste. Shape into small balls and cook them in boiling salted water for 15 minutes then add to your soup.

GREEN-PEAS SOUP
(Elizabeth Raffald, 1769)

SHELL a peck of peas, and boil them in spring-water* till they are soft, then work them through a hair-sieve. Take the water that your peas were boiled in, and put in a knuckle of veal, three slices of ham, and cut two carrots, a turnip, and a few beet leaves. Shred small, add a little more water to the meat, set it over the fire, and let it boil one hour and a half; then strain the gravy into a bowl, and mix it with the pulp, and put in a little juice of spinage, which must be beat and squeezed through a cloth, put in as much as will make it look a pretty colour, then give it a gentle boil, which will take off the taste of the spinage (spinach), slice in the whitest part of a head of celery, put in a lump of sugar the size of a walnut, take a slice of bread, and cut it in little square pieces, cut a little bacon the same way, fry them a little brown in fresh butter, cut a large cabbage-lettuce in slices, fry it after the other, put it in the tureen with fried bread and bacon; have ready boiled, as for eating, a pint of young peas, and put them in the soup, with a little chopped mint if you like it, and pour it into your tureen.

Chapter 5

FISH

When it came to having fish in the Northern Counties, economy was the name of the game. Fish Pies and Fish Cakes were in abundance along with fresh water fish bakes not forgetting ye good ole fish & chips. Having the sea to both the east & west, fishing in the area is well established, having masses of white fish such as plaice, whiting, haddock and cod. From the northern waters we can catch crabs, scallops and lobsters, not forgetting the brown shrimp which made the Morecambe Bay Potted Shrimp famous from the west coast. We have some of the finest fish markets in the North, the best by far being in the Lancashire area, thanks to Fleetwood Morecambe & Grimsby where you can get every type of fish that is available in Europe. Our rivers and lakes are also plentiful with Brown Trout, Pike and the very unique Char.

There is not very much known about the char, which is a member of the salmon family, confined in the very deep areas of the lakes but is very common in the Windermere area.

LOBSTER SOUFFLE
(Lyn Wilkinson)

275g (10 oz) cooked and finely chopped Lobster meat
250ml (9 fl oz) Milk
2 shallots, finely chopped
1 bay leaf
4 black & 4 pink peppercorns
1 sprig of thyme & thyme sprigs for garnish
1 pinch of freshly chopped tarragon
1 pinch of cayenne pepper
freshly grated nutmeg
4 eggs, separated
15g (½oz) plain flour
2 tablespoons natural yoghurt
40g butter
1 lemon sliced

Pre-heat your oven at Gas Mark 7, 425F (220c).

Into a saucepan put the milk, peppercorns and bayleaf, bring them to the boil. Remove from the heat and let it infuse for 15 minutes. Strain through a wire sieve.

In a separate saucepan, place the chopped shallots with the butter, cooking until the shallots are soft not browned.

Add the sifted flour and cook for two minutes on a low heat.

Remove from the heat and gradually add the warmed milk, bring the milk to the boil. Leave to cool before blending in the egg yolks and yoghurt, adding also the pieces of freshly cooked lobster seasoning well with the herbs.

Whisk the egg whites until peaked, folding them into the mixture.

Spoon into a buttered souffle dish and bake in the oven for upto 15 minutes. Garnish the souffle on serving with slices of fresh lemon and thyme.

LANCASHIRE STUFFED TROUT
(Peter Reid)

This is a recipe I made for a friend of mine, Peter Reid, who is now Manager of Manchester City Football Club. This recipe is over 120 years old.

I used to serve this to Peter, when I was in the restaurant business in Bolton.

275g (10 oz) X 4 water trout,
(gutted & cleaned)
8 pieces of rindless streaky bacon.
100g (4 oz) fresh breadcrumbs
1 small onion, skinned and finely chopped
25g (1 oz) crushed almonds
1 egg beaten
5ml (1 tsp) English mustard
5ml (1 tsp) mixed herbs
10ml (1 tbsp) White wine
10ml (1 tbsp) garlic oil
salt & pepper
freshly chopped chives
lemon wedges

Put the breadcrumbs, white wine, mustard, garlic oil, beaten egg and crushed almonds into a bowl and mix well together and season.

Fill the cavities of the trout with the stuffing. Wrap in the streaky bacon and place on a greased baking tray (sheet) and bake for 20 minutes at Gas 6, 200c, 400f.

Sprinkle with freshly chopped chives, garnished with lemon wedges.

HEYSHAM FISH PIE
(Ted Weaver, Makro)

350g/12 oz cooked white fish
225g/8 oz mashed potatoes
25g/1 oz butter
25g/1 oz plain flour
25g/1 oz grated Lancashire cheese
275ml/ half pint of milk
2 eggs separated
salt
freshly ground black pepper

Make a sauce with the butter, flour, milk and cheese. Bring to the boil in a saucepan over a gentle heat. When thickened, add the cooked fish and mashed potatoes. Add salt and pepper to taste, then the beaten egg yolks and simmer until all are slightly cooked. Then add the stiffly beaten egg whites and pour into a greased pie dish. Bake in a pre-heated oven for 20 minutes at Gas 5, 190c (375F).

COD & CHIPS
(The Walnut Tree, Bootle)

Fish & Chips have been a northern tradition for over 120 years.

It started with the street sellers and we have had the burden of having them for lunch and dinner ever since. I remember it being sold in newspapers, but the hygiene laws have now prevented it.

I had the pleasure of having one of the best meals of breaded plaice with home-made chips & peas served to me by Julie Benson in her mother Wyn Godfrey's pub the Walnut Tree in Bootle.

4 pieces of fresh cod, filleted, skin left on
1 kg potatoes peeled & chipped
vegetable oil & pan for deep frying

BATTER

200g/7 oz plain flour
1 egg
water & milk
salt & pepper

To make the batter mix the flour, salt, pepper, egg in a bowl, beating in the milk and water until the mixture is about the consistency of single cream. Leave it to stand for 1 hour.

Heat the oil until it gives off a faint, almost invisible, blue smoke (180C, 350F). Fry the chips in small batches, when they start to brown remove with a small slotted spoon or if you use a basket, the basket. Put the chips into a warm oven.

Dip each piece of fish into the batter, drawing it backwards and forwards 2 to 3 times to coat it fully. Then lower it gently into the hot fat, with the skin side down to prevent it curling. Fry them one at a time. After 5 minutes turn the fish over cooking until brown for about 8 to 10 minutes.

Serve on Newspaper with salt and vinegar.

HADDOCK FISH CAKES
(Bill Moreland)

Housewives of the north could only afford to spend very little during the war and this very economical way of making fish go further is still popular today.

275g/10 oz Haddock, skinned and boned
350g/12 ozs cooked potatoes, mashed
10ml/2 tablespoons best butter, softened
15ml/1 tablespoon chives
15ml/1 tablespoon parsley
50ml/2 fl oz milk, blended with 1 egg
50g/2 oz fresh breadcrumbs
50ml/ 2 fl oz double cream
salt and pepper

Blend together the fish with the potatoes, chives, parsley, butter, egg and cream, either do this by hand, blender or food processor, seasoning well.

Shape the mixture into 4 to 6 fish cakes coated with the breadcrumbs.

Grill or fry in a light vegetable oil for 4 minutes either side until golden brown.

BAKED MACKEREL
(Melanie Eves)

4 Mackerel about 350g/12 ozs,
cleaned and heads removed
25g/1 oz butter
salt and pepper
lemon juice

Season the mackerel inside and out with salt
and pepper and lemon juice. Make three
slashes into the skin on each side of the fish,
rub over with the butter and grill for 15-20
minutes, turning once until tender.

Pour over the juices and serve with lemon.

KIPPER SOUFFLE
(Jeremy Rata, Crest Hotel, Preston)

If it was not for Jeremy saying to me
'Tom why not FI-FO'. I did and the result
was this book.

350g/12 ozs Cooked Manx Kippers,
bones and skin removed
25g/1 oz butter
25g/1 oz plain flour
300ml/half pint of milk
2 egg separated
salt
fresh ground black pepper

Mash the kippers. Melt the butter in a
saucepan and stir in the flour. Cook for 2
minutes, stirring.

Remove from the heat.

Gradually add the milk, stirring well after
each addition.

Return to the heat and mix in the mashed
kippers. Add salt, if necessary, and plenty of
pepper. Remove from the heat and stir the
egg yolks into the mixture. Whisk the egg
whites until they form stiff peaks and then
fold them into the mixture slowly.

Turn into a lightly buttered souffle dish or
deep dish and bake in a pre-heated oven Gas
6, 200c (400F) for 25 minutes.

CRISPY SAWLEY SALMON BAKE
(Peggy & Gerry, Westhoughton)

Quick and simple, this is yet again
combining the use of Lancashire cheese
with a crisp flavour of Kellog's.

350g/12 oz cooked salmon
or tinned salmon 200g/8 ozs
cooked and mashed potatoes with butter
350ml/12 fl oz milk and cream
50g/2 oz Lancashire cheese, crumbled
2 eggs
100g/4 ozs crushed cornflakes
salt
pepper

Flake the salmon with a fork, discarding the
bones and skin, and place in a casserole dish.

Beat together the eggs, cream and milk, add
the cheese & potatoes, roughly blend into the
salmon. Sprinkle with the crushed cornflakes
and bake in a pre-heated moderate oven at
Gas 4 180c (350F) for 20 minutes.

To boil a PIKE
with a pudding in the belly.
(Mrs Raffald, 1769)

TAKE out the gills and guts, wash it well, then make a good force-meat of oysters chopped fine, the crumbs of half a penny loaf, a few sweet herbs, and a little lemon-peel shred fine, nutmeg, pepper, and salt, to your taste, a good lump of butter, the yolks of two eggs, mix them well-together, and put them in the belly of your fish, sew it up, skewer it round, put hard water in your fish-pan, add to it a tea-cupful of vinegar, and a little salt: when it boils put in the fish: if it be a middle size, it will take half an hour's boiling; garnish it with walnuts and pickled barberries; serve it up with oyster-sauce in a boat, and pour a little sauce on the pike. You may dress a roasted pike the same way.

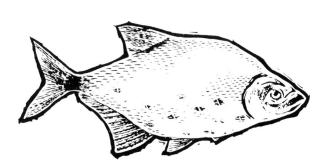

A VERY OLD LANCASHIRE FISH PIE
(Bill & Pat Scafe)

For this dish you can use either cod or haddock, I always use cod. You can also use the suet pastry recipe on page (26) or use mashed potatoes for the topping, I again prefer the potato topping.

450g (1lb) cod fillet (small bones removed)
300ml (half pint) Thwaites beer
1 tin of chopped tomatoes
1 large onion chopped finely
150ml (¼ pint) basic cheese sauce
450g (1lb) mashed potatoes with cream
& butter
125g (4 oz) grated cheddar cheese
Salt & freshly ground black pepper

Place the beer in a large frying pan and poach the fish for 15 minutes until cooked.

Then place the fish and beer stock into a large mixing bowl and blend with the chopped tomatoes, onion and basic cheese sauce.

Season well with salt and pepper and place into a deep casserole.
Top with mashed potato and finish with the grated cheese.

Bake in t oven for 25 minutes at Gas 7, 425f, 220c

Serve with crusty bread and a pint of real ale

If you have never had this in Lancashire you have never lived.

Chapter 6

POTTED DISHES

The tradition of Potting food started in the early 16th century and was introduced from the North for the travellers, when the cooks began to preserve fish and meat for long journeys throughout Britain.

All Potted dishes can be very easily made today using a Blender. During the turn of the century they were made by using a pestle & mortar, fork or hand whisk. Should you not have available a blender, then do use in the traditional method.

Potted dishes are still popular in the north because they are cheap and easy for sandwiches, quick snacks and salads. Here are several which I am sure you would like to try yourself, because they are very easy to make and extremely economical.

Using again all the cheap cuts of cooked meat, fish and vegetables or any expensive left-overs this section will save you a great deal of money and give a lesson in food wastage.

When potting meat and fish, you would use a great deal of clarified butter, with this in mind this is how you would do it.

CLARIFIED BUTTER

Use 225g (8 ozs) of butter, which will produce about 175g (2ozs) of clarified butter. Place the butter in a small saucepan and heat very slowly, skimming off the foam as the butter heats.

Sediment sinks to the bottom of the pan as the butter heats. When completely melted remove the pan from the heat and leave to stand for 4 minutes. Then strain the butter through cheesecloth or fine cotton into a bowl. Allow the butter to cool a little before pouring it over the surface of the potted product you are using.

POTTED BEEF
(Elizabeth RAFFALD, Salford, 1760)
Original Recipe.

Take three or four pounds, or any smaller quantity, of lean beef, free from sinews, and rub it well with a mixture made of a handful of salt, one ounce of saltpetre, and one ounce of course sugar; let the meat lie in the salt for two days, turning and rubbing it twice a day. Put it into a stone jar with a little beef gravy, and cover it with a paste to keep it close. Bake it for several hours in a very slow oven till the meat is tender; then pour off the gravy, which should be in a very small quantity, or the juice of the meat will be lost; pound the meat, when cold, in a marble mortar till it is reduced to a smooth paste, adding by degrees a little fresh butter melted. Season it as you proceed with pepper, allspice, nutmeg, pounded mace, and cloves, or such of these spices as are thought agreeable. Some flavour with anchovy, ham, shallots, mustard, wine, flavoured vinegar, ragout powder, curry powder, &c., according to taste.

When it is thoroughly beaten and mingled together, press it closely into small shallow pots, nearly full and fill them up with a layer a quarter of an inch thick of clarified butter, and tie them up with a bladder, or sheet of Indian rubber. They should be kept in a cool place.

N.B. Just think of the work involved in the above recipe. I have made this recipe and I can assure you it is worthwhile, but very hard work. T.B.

MARBLED HAM
(Christine Thacker, Preston)

It is well known the Georgians loved Marbled meats for the colour and design and this without exception was one of the favourites, dating back to 1790.

All the following meats need to be thoroughly cooked and then left to go cold.

450g (1lb) cold York ham
225g (½lb) cold tongue
225g (½lb) cold veal
1½ teaspoons of ground mace

225g (8 oz) Clarified Butter (see recipe)
275g (10 oz) Softened butter
Salt
Freshly ground black pepper
Waxed paper (greaseproof)

Mince the Veal finely and pound to a paste. Beat in a quarter of the softened butter and season with a little mace, pepper & salt.

Place to one side. Repeat the same process with the tongue.

Using the rest of the softened butter, repeat the process with the ham.

Into a souffle dish (1 pint) completely cover the bottom of the dish with a thick layer of the ham paste. Then dot lumps of veal & tongue paste all over the top. Repeating this process and ending with a layer of ham. Cover with waxed paper, and weight the top with heavy tin or flat heavy object. Chill in the refrigerator over night.

Remove the weight and paper, and seal with clarified butter. Put it back into the refrigerator to set completely (2 hours) cold before serving. Cut into small wedges to show the 'marbling'.

Serve it with a fresh crisp salad & hot fingers of toast.

CHICKEN LIVER PASTE
(Betty & Bill, The Lion, Atherton)

450g (1 lb) Chicken Livers
100g (4 oz) Best butter
3 tablespoons medium sherry
1 teaspoon grated ginger
salt
Freshly ground black pepper
2 tablespoon double cream
Clarified butter (see recipe 000)

Blend together in a glass or china bowl, the ginger, salt and freshly ground black pepper and leave this to stand for four hours. Chop the liver roughly. Melt the butter in a non-stick frying pan, adding the livers. Cook them slowly for 5 minutes.

Then mash or blend them with the sherry & double cream cook for a further 2 minutes allow to cool, taste and season if required. Pot and seal with clarified butter.

POTTED SMOKED TROUT
(Yvonne & Simon Wildi, Newburgh)

This very likeable recipe has been popular in Newburgh for over 60 years. The recipe used to be made with Char which are very scarce today, the Char being very popular for over 200 years. Char which was once plentiful had a delicate pink, salmon-like flesh and was also popular oven baked or wrapped in a puff pastry case.

8 fillets of smoked trout
(skinned and deboned)
a pinch of grated nutmeg & mace
100g (4 ozs) butter, softened
salt
freshly ground black pepper
2 tablespoons port
2 tablespoons double cream
clarified butter (see recipe 000)

Place the fillets into a large bowl with all the ingredients except the clarified butter.

Pound until very smooth and pot, cover with a waxed paper and weight. Place in the refrigerator for 4 hours. Remove and seal with the clarified butter, place back into the refrigerator for 1 day. Serve with toast & lemon wedges.

POTTED SMOKED MACKEREL PATE
(Karen Chesterfield)

3 fillets of smoked mackerel,
deboned & skinned
250g/8 ozs Creamed Cheese with chives
150ml/5 floz soured cream
1 teaspoon English mustard
fresh ground black pepper

Mash the mackerel in a bowl with a fork, gradually blend in the cheese, soured cream, mustard and freshly milled black pepper.

You can use a blender or food processor should you wish.

Blend until it is completely smooth. Pack into individual dishes and chill thoroughly for 1 hour before serving with lemon wedges and hot fingers of toast.

POTTED TONGUE
(Steven Wolsey, Standish)

A fellow chef told me what he does with his leftovers from a cooked tongue and everyday things around the house.

175g/6 oz cooked tongue, minced
20g/2 ozs cooked ham, finely chopped
50g/2 ozs cooked chicken livers,
finely chopped
15ml/1 tablespoon of chunky marmalade
15ml/1 tablespoon of branston pickle
1 pinch of nutmeg
1 pinch of cayenne
125g/4 oz clarified butter (see recipe)
Freshly milled pepper

Place all the ingredients except the clarified butter into a large bowl and pound it until it is completely mixed together and smooth. Or place in a food blender or processor until smooth.

Place into individual pots, covering each pot with a thin layer of clarified butter.

Original recipe I have from 1845 for Potted Ox-tongue. One pound and a half of boiled tongue; six ounces of butter; a little Cayenne; a small spoonful of pounded mace; nutmeg and cloves.

Cut about a pound and a half from an unsmoked boiled tongue, remove the rind. Pound it in a mortar as fine as possible with butter, and the spices beaten fine. When perfectly pounded, and the spice well blended with the meat, press it into small potting-pans, pour clarified butter over the top.

A little roast veal added to the potted tongue is an improvement.

One of the most popular meats of the north, during the war and the recession, rationing etc. was the rabbit. Today it is not so popular. In 1868 Potted Rabbit was a delicacy and was popular with the gentry. From *Warnes Model Cookery* of that year, I show you how they would Pot a Rabbit.

TO POT RABBITS
(Mary Jewry 1868)

Two or three young rabbits
pepper
mace
a little Cayenne
salt
allspice
and a large piece of butter.

Cut up and wash two or three young but full-grown rabbits, and take the legs of at the thigh. Pack them as closely as possible in a small pan after seasoning them with pepper and salt, mace, all spice, and a very little Cayenne, all in fine powder.

Make the top as smooth as you can, keep out the heads and carcasses, but take of the meat from the neck.

Put in a good deal of butter, and bake whole gently for two hours, keep it two days in a pan, then shift it into small pots, adding butter. The livers also may be added, as they eat well.

POTTED PIGEONS ALA BOWTON

(Author's recipe)
Converted by the author and translated from the
1769 recipe of Elizabeth
Raffald's cookbook.

This is quite a nice recipe, if you have the patience.

3 pigeons
250g/8 oz butter, softened
30ml/2 tablespoons of brandy
30ml/2 tablespoons sherry
8 juniper berries, crushed
a pinch of mace, nutmeg and cinnamon
1 crushed clove of garlic
150g/5 oz onions, finely chopped
9 pieces of rindless streaky bacon
freshly milled pepper
salt

With 175g/6 ozs softened butter, blend in the juniper berries, mace, nutmeg, garlic, cinnamon and onions.

Cover and fill each bird with the spicy butter. Wrap three pieces of streaky bacon around each bird and place them breast downwards, in medium sized lidded casserole.

Add 1 tablespoon of brandy and the sherry cover the birds with the lid and cook for 2 hours at Gas 3 160C (350F) for 2 hours.

Remove the pieces of bacon carefully and put to one side. Strip the meat off the birds while they are hot. Pouring the liquor from the birds into a small bowl and leave it to cool until the butter solidifies. Line a pot with three pieces of the cooked bacon and pack in one-third of the pigeon meat, which should be finely chopped, pressing down firmly. Repeat the process until the pot as three strips of bacon on the top.

Take the butter off the cooking liquor, and scrape away any bits of meat. Bring it just to melting point add the brandy and pour over the pigeons.

Clarify the remaining butter (see recipe) and seal the potted pigeons. I always serve this dish after three days to give it time to marinade in its own juices, It should keep in a fridge for at least 1 month.

Chapter 7

CHEESE & CHEESE DISHES

Northern cookery is based on dishes that are suitable for a hard-working community in a bracing climate, simple, cheap and tasty meals at the minimum of cost. And cheese covers every aspect of that. Lancashire, Yorkshire and Cumbria between them encompass huge tracts of land. Two and half million litres of milk a year are produced in the area, which much of this is used to produce the delicious cheeses for which our region is famous.

LANCASHIRE is the most readily recognised cheese in the North. A crumbly, white cheese, slightly salty, with a full-bodied flavour. The richer farmhouse version usually uses unpasteurised milk. The cheese is the softest of English pressed cheeses and melts very well, so is ideal for toasting and cooking.

WENSLEYDALE until the 1920s, always had blue veins. However, these days the white version is more common and the veined cheese is now known as Blue Wensleydale. French monks who founded the great abbeys in the Yorkshire Dales, following the Norman Conquest of 1066, first brought the recipe to this country. The cheese was made at Jervaulx Abbey by the Cistercians, although in those times ewes' milk was used. It wasn't until after the 16th century, when the monasteries were dissolved and production moved to local farmhouses and dairies, that cows' milk was introduced into the recipe. The North Country way to eat Wensleydale is with a slice of apple pie, gingerbread or fruit cake.

Wensleydale is usually eaten young. This white cheese with a close, smooth texture is mild with a refreshing flavour.

COTHERSTONE is another cheese, originally made by monks, which is enjoying a revival today. It is not widely available, since it is made only by a small number of producers in Yorkshire. Made in a white or blue-veined version, from unpasteurised milk, Cotherstone cheese is open-textured with a sharp, slightly acidic flavour. It develops a natural crust, similar to Camembert, which changes from gold to pink as it ages.

CHEESE AND CHIVE SCONES
(Paul Yeo, Lancashire 1923)

Crumbly Lancashire cheese is ideal for cooking. Combined with the onion flavour of fresh chives, these scones are a delicious snack.

100g (4 oz) Lancashire cheese, grated
225g (8oz) self-raising flour
50g (2oz) butter, softened
160ml fresh milk, saving some for brushing
15ml (1 tbsp) snipped fresh chives
pinch of salt

Pre-heat the oven at Gas 8, 450f, 230C.

Into a large bowl put the flour and salt and rub this into the softened butter until the mixture resembles fine breadcrumbs.

Stir in 50g of the cheese and the chives, add the milk and mix to form a soft dough, then knead quickly until smooth.

Roll out the mixture, on a floured work surface until 1 cm (1/2 inch) in thickness . Cut into 10 rounds with a 5cm (2 inch) plain or ridged cutter and brush the tops with the leftover milk (10ml) Transfer to a greased baking sheet. Bake in the oven for 10 minutes until well risen and golden brown.

Immediately put the remaining cheese on the top of the scones and allow the cheese to melt before serving them hot with clotted cream and Jam.

LANCASHIRE, MACARONI & BROCCOLI CHEESE
(Sue & John Melia)

100g (4 oz) Lancashire cheese, grated
100g (4 oz) broccoli florets
75g (3 oz) wholewheat macaroni
25g (1 oz) butter
25g (1 oz) plain flour , sifted
300ml (½ pint) fresh milk
15ml (1 tbsp)
fresh wholemeal breadcrumbs
5ml (1 tsp) freshly chopped tarragon
salt & pepper

Into 1.1 litres of boiling salted water put the macaroni, cooking for 15 minutes then drain it.

Into another saucepan, but the butter, flour and milk, whisking continuously, until the sauce is smooth. Remove the pan from the heat, add 75g (3 oz) of the cheese and stir until melted. Season and add the freshly chopped tarragon.

Blanch the broccoli in the base of a large casserole or flameproof serving dish. Cover with the macaroni and cheese sauce. Sprinkle with the remaining 25g (1 oz) cheese and breadcrumbs. brown under a hot grill.

QUICK MANCHESTER RAREBIT
(Fran & David Hall)

What makes a good Lancashire rarebit is beer. This typical British dish has been mentioned in several old cookery books.

225g (½ lb) Lancashire cheese
50g (2 ozs) fresh breadcrumbs
4 Tablespoons of double cream
3 Tablespoons of Traditional Beer
1 teaspoon of old English mustard
salt
freshly ground black pepper
4 slices of wholemeal or hovis bread, toasted

Put all the ingredients into a non-stick saucepan and bring to the boil slowly, stirring all the time. Let it simmer for 2 minutes, continue to stir until it thickens. Pour onto the toast and grill very quickly.

PAN HAGGERTY
(Tony Ashton)

Pan Haggerty is a dish known as knock -up , the term coming from the boozy men of the north after a night at the pub, would shout ''Ma mak us some nok up.'' It was cheap and cheerful food, knowing after 30 minutes, he would be fast asleep, but the Pan Haggerty could be re-used the following day.

100g (4 oz) Cheddar or Lancashire Cheese
50g (2 oz) butter
15ml (1 tbsp) vegetable oil
2 medium onions, skinned and thinly sliced
450g (1lb) potatoes, peeled & thinly sliced
(Maris Pipers)
salt & fresh pepper

Heat the butter & oil in a large heavy non-stick frying pan.

Remove from the heat and interlaying the onions, potato and cheese, ending with a top layer of cheese. Cover and cook on a medium heat for 30 minutes.

Uncover and grill for the last 4 minutes.

LANCASHIRE CHEESE SOUFFLE
(Sarah & Marc Davies)

100g/4 ozs grated Lancashire Cheese
50g/2 oz butter
50g/2 oz plain flour (sifted)
200ml/7 fl oz fresh milk
30ml/2 tablespoons single cream
salt
Freshly milled pepper
2 large eggs separated

Put the butter, sifted flour, milk and cream in a saucepan. Heat, whisking continuously, until the sauce thickens and is smooth in texture, simmer for 2 minutes. Remove the pan from the heat, add the cheese, stirring until it is completely melted. Season with salt and freshly milled pepper.

Beat in the egg yolks. Whisk the egg whites until stiff and peaky, fold into the mixture very slowly with a metal spoon.

Pour the mixture into a large greased souffle dish and bake in a pre-heated oven gas 5, 190c (350F) for 30 minutes until well risen and golden brown.

I serve this straight from the oven with home-made wholemeal bread and butter.

CHEESE RAMEKINS
(Sean O'Callaghan)

50g/2 ozs Lancashire Cheese, grated
50g/2 ozs Cheshire Cheese
50g/2 oz cooked ham, finely chopped
30ml/ 2 tablespoons freshly chopped chives
60ml/ 4 tablespoons single cream
50g/ 2 oz fresh breadcrumbs
2 eggs separated
salt
freshly milled pepper

Put the cheese, ham, cream, chives and breadcrumbs into a bowl blending them all together season to taste.

Grease 6 ramekin dishes and place them onto a baking sheet. Beat the egg yolks into the mixture. Whisk the egg whites until stiff and peaky, then with a metal spoon fold them very slowly into the mixture. Spoon the mixture into the ramekin dishes and bake in a pre-heated oven at Gas mark 6, 200c (400f) for 15 minutes.

CHEESE AND POTATO CAKES
(Dave Crompton)

This is one of the most popular dishes at tea-time in Lancashire, served with egg and chips, with lashings of tomato sauce.

50g/2 ozs Cheddar Cheese
50g/2 ozs Plain flour
50g/2 ozs butter
50g/2 ozs minced cooked ham
350g/12 ozs mashed potato
1 teaspoon dry English mustard
1 egg beaten
salt
freshly milled pepper

Beat the softened butter into the mashed potato, blending in the cheese, mustard powder, flour, ham and egg, making sure it is completed mixed and seasoned. Drop large spoonfuls into a greased non-stick frying pan or a hot griddle. Cook for 5 minutes either side. Serve with eggs or on their own.

CHEESE & ONION PIE
in the Traditional manner
1928 (Nicola McPherson)

500g/1 lb Shortcrust pastry (using recipe 000)
225g/8 ozs Cheddar Cheese
225g/8 ozs potatoes cooked and cut into small cubes
1 large onion, finely chopped
45ml/3 tablespoons milk
45ml/3 tablespoons cream
1 large egg, whisked with a little cream
100g/4 oz sliced button mushroom (optional)
salt
freshly milled pepper

Roll out the pastry and line a greased pie dish.

Blend all the above ingredients together, seasoning well and place into the pastry case. Top with a pastry lid, egg wash and bake in a pre-heated oven Gas Mark 6 for 25 minutes until the top is crisp and golden brown.

ONIONS AND CHEESE
1830 (Reg & Margaret Syddal)

This is a Lancashire (Bolton-le-Moors) Sunday supper dish eaten with slices of currant bread.

2 Onions
1 pint milk
salt
1 lb grated cheese

Boil the onions in milk, when done drain but do not drain to dry. Chop them up and stir grated cheese in them. Return to pan, reheat, then serve.

CHEESE STRAWS 1895
(Rose & Dave Walton, Edge Tavern, Astley Bridge)

Use puff paste and Lancashire cheese. Roll out the paste and cut into pieces about three inches long and an inch and a half wide.

Cut thin strips of the cheese a little less than three inches long and half an inch wide. Place these on the pastry, moisten with white of egg and roll the pastry over the cheese. Brush over with milk and bake for ten minutes in the oven or fry in hot fat.

To Stew CHEESE with LIGHT WIGGS
(Elizabeth Raffald, 1769)

CUT a plateful of cheese, pour on it a glass of red wine, stew it before the fire, toast a light wigg, (crumpet) pour over it two or three spoonfuls of hot red wine, put it in the middle of your dish, lay the cheese over it; and serve it up.

To Stew CHEESE
1769

CUT your cheese very thin, lay it in a toaster, set it before the fire, pour a glass of ale over it, let it stand till it is like a light custard, then pour it on toasts or wiggs, and send it in hot.

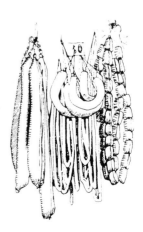

63

Chapter 8

VEGETABLE RECIPES

Sir Walter Raleigh has generally been attributed the introduction of the potato into England in 1586, but the fact is Sir Francis Drake brought them into this country a year before, just 20 years after they had been taken into Ireland by Sir John Hawkins. Besides being in themselves a most useful and indispensable food, potatoes are the most common vegetable in use in British kitchens today.

I recently had the pleasure of dining in a superb restaurant in Dalton, Lancashire called Prescotts Restaurant & Country Hotel which is run by Cesare & Angela Marchesan. The vegetables that they presented with my main course was a delight to see. It had the touch of going back in time, with presentation of a very high standard.

CREAMED LEEKS WITH GARLIC CHEESE & CHIVES
(Cesare Marchesan)

450g (1 lb) young leeks, trimmed & finely shredded
2 cloves of garlic crushed
25g (1 oz) of chives finely snipped
25g (1 oz) butter
2 tbsp thick cream
2 tbsp grated cheddar cheese
salt & freshly ground black pepper

Wash & drain the leeks. Melt the butter in a large non-stick frying pan , add the leeks and simmer with a lid on the pan for 2 minutes. Add the cheese, garlic, chives and cream, season lightly cooking for a further two minutes and place in a hot serving dish.

The most popular vegetables recipe besides mushy peas and chips are the colly cheesebake & baked parsnip and carrot. I have restyled the recipes from the method of 1834 to the taste of the 1990,s.

CAULIFLOWER CHEESE
(Derek Billington)

large white cauliflower, broken into 2.5 cm
(1 inch) florets
150ml (quarter pint) single cream
2 heap tablespoon of Parmesan cheese
1 quarter teaspoon of ground mace
1 small clove of garlic, crushed with a little
lemon juice
1 teaspoon of lemon juice
freshly ground black pepper

Place the cheese, cream, mace and garlic into
a non-stick sauce-pan, thoroughly blending
together and let it stand for 3 hours, stirring
every hour. Using NO heat at all.

Place the cauliflower florets into boiling
salted water, adding the lemon juice and a
little milk (keeps the florets pure white), cook
for 3 minutes. Drain well. Place the florets
into the cream mixture and cook over a
medium heat. place into a serving dish top
with a little more parmesan and grill for 1
minute.

PEASE PUDDING

Pease pudding hot, pease pudding cold,
Pease pudding in the pot, nine days old.

450g/1lb Split peas
1 large potato, peeled and diced
1.2 ltr/2 pints of bacon or ham stock
salt
freshly milled pepper

Wash the peas, mix with the potato. Place
them together into a muslin bag and tie it up
loosely. Place into a saucepan, cover with the
bacon or ham stock. Bring to the boil and
simmer for 2 hours. Remove the saucepan
and remove the muslin bag very carefully
from the stock, allow it to drain for 2
minutes. Empty the contents into a bowl and
mash to a pulp, adding a little stock to
moisten.

VEGETABLE HOT-POT

This recipe was taught me by Eric Shaw,
when I was living in Newton-le-Willows.

450g/1lb Potatoes, peeled and sliced thinly
3 Carrots, peeled and sliced
3 Parsnips, peeled and sliced
1 Turnip, peeled and sliced
2 Onions, peeled and sliced
2 Leeks, thinly sliced
4 large tomatoes, skinned, deseeded
and chopped
100g/ 4 oz Mushrooms, sliced
100g/ 4 oz green beans, topped and tailed
4 celery stalks, cut into thick matchsticks
600ml/ 1 pint of chicken stock
Freshly ground black pepper
1 bay leaf
1 tablespoon chopped parsley
1 teaspoon chopped thyme
1 teaspoon sweet herbs

Place all the ingredients into a large
flameproof casserole, bring to the boil, skim
off, then top with the slices of potato cook
gently for 30 minutes, until all the vegetables
are tender.

65

POTATO CAKES
(Janice McGrath, Salford)

450g/1lb Cooked potato, mashed
and seasoned
25g/1 oz finely chopped onion
1 egg beaten with a little milk
flour
cooking oil

Mix all the ingredients together, making sure
the mixture does not become to moist. Shape
into little flat cakes.

Put a little cooking oil into a frying pan,
cooking the cakes on both sides until golden
brown.

BAKED POTATO & ONION
(Dave & Jan, Peel Monument, Radcliffe.)

5 medium potatoes, peeled and finely sliced
5 medium onions, peeled and finely sliced
pinch of nutmeg
freshly milled pepper
salt
175ml/6 fl oz milk
4 tablespoons vegetable stock

Alternate the potatoes and onion slices in a
shallow ovenproof dish, seasoning each layer.
Pour over the stock and milk.

Cover and bake in a pre-heated oven at Gas
Mark 6, 200C/400f for about 45 minutes until
the potatoes are cooked. Uncover to allow
the top to brown, cooking for a further 5
minutes.

CABBAGE & APPLE BAKE
*(Charles Thomas & Carol Davies,
Walkden)*

This is a recipe I always serve with Pork
or as a Vegetarian alternative. This is the
stuff that helps keep you healthy and
spot free, I also recommend this recipe in
professional footballers diets.

1 small white cabbage, finely shredded
1 large Onion, peeled, finely sliced
3 large Granny Smith apples, peeled
and grated
150ml/quarter pint of Orange Juice
150ml/quarter pint of soured cream
2 tablespoons vegetable stock
1 clove garlic peeled and crushed
1 tablespoon caraway seeds
Salt and freshly milled pepper
freshly chopped parsley.

Place the cabbage, onion and apples in layers
in a baking dish.

Blend the garlic and caraway seeds with the
orange juice and vegetable stock and pour
over the vegetables and cover.

Bake in a pre-heated oven Gas Mark 6, 200c/
400f for 30 minutes.
Uncover and pour over the seasoned sour
cream and blend in thoroughly. Reduce the
oven to Gas 4 ,180c/350f and cook for a
further 10 minutes.

Sprinkle with freshly chopped parsley.

CELERY CHEESE
(Janet McGreggor)

1 head of celery, finely sliced
75g/3 oz grated cheese
milk
1 egg beaten
fresh breadcrumbs
salt
freshly milled pepper

Place the celery in a saucepan and barely
cover with milk. Season well and simmer
until the celery is cooked. Allow it to cool
and blend in the cheese and egg. Place the
mixture into a greased pie-dish, cover with
the fresh breadcrumbs and cook at Gas 4,
350f/180c until golden brown.

SALFORD THATCH

This recipe was usually served at tea-
time with sausages, egg and tomatoes. I
have a feeling this is a transformation of
Elizabeth Raffald's recipe from 1769.

225g/8 oz grated raw potato
225g/8 oz chopped bacon (fat removed)
50g/2 oz plain flour, seasoned
2 large eggs, beaten.
1 tablespoon cream

Blend all the ingredients together, Melt
enough dripping to cover the bottom of a
large frying pan. When the dripping is hot,
spread the mixture evenly over the base of
the pan and cook gently until crisp and
brown on the base and completely set on the
top. Turn and cook the other side until crisp
and brown. Cut into wedges and serve.

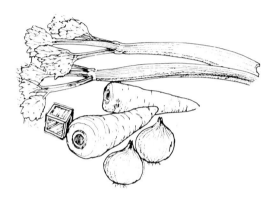

STUFFED ONIONS
(Kenny Ratcliffe, Manchester)

4 medium size onions, skin removed
75g/3 ozs grated cheese
75g/3 ozs fresh breadcrumbs
a large pinch of dry English mustard
butter
salt and freshly milled pepper

Boil the onions for 15 minutes. Combine the
mustard, cheese and breadcrumbs in a bowl.
Scoop out the centres of the cooked onions
and blend them with the ingredients in the
bowl, seasoning well. Stuff the onions with
the mixture. Place the onions on a greased
ovenproof dish, topped with a little butter
and cook in a pre-heated oven Gas 7, 425f/
220c for 25 minutes.

STUMP

My lad's Gareth and Matty, hate
vegetables, but when I serve this with
the Sunday roast they are completely
STUMPED!

225g/8 oz carrot, peeled and sliced
225g/8 oz potatoes, peeled and sliced
225g/8 oz swede, peeled and sliced
25g/1 oz best butter
150ml/quarter pint of fresh milk
1 tablespoon double cream
salt
freshly milled pepper

Simmer the vegetables in lightly seasoned
water for 30 minutes until soft. Drain them
well.

Mash the vegetables with the butter, milk
and cream, check the seasoning, reheat
gently and serve.

To ragoo MUSHROOMS
(Elizabeth Raffald, 1769)

TAKE large mushrooms, peel, and take out
the inside, broil them in a gridiron, when the
outside is brown put them into a tossing pan,
with as much water as will cover them, let
them stand ten minutes, then put to them a
spoonful of white wine, the same of
browning, a very little allegar, thicken it with
flour and butter, boil it a little, lay sippets
round your dish, and serve it up.

Chapter 9

POULTRY AND GAME

We have poultry and Game in abundance in the north, with Mackentie a major poultry suppliers on my doorstep and Openshaws the best and biggest suppliers of Game in Lancashire, what we do not have is silly prices like they have in the south.

Elizabeth Raffald supplied game dishes to order from her emporium in Old Exchange Alley, Manchester and served them in her pubs the King's Head, Salford and the Bull's Head in the Market Place.

Here are a selection of Mrs Raffald's original recipes for your enjoyment from 1750 to 1769.

You will note the f is used for the letter S during this period of writing.

To roaft
PHEASANTS or PARTRIDGES

WHEN you roaft pheafants or partridges, keep them at a good diftance from the fire, duft them, and bafte them often with frefh butter; if your fire is good, half an hour will roaft them; put a little gravy in your difh, made of a fcrag of mutton, a fpoonful of catchup, the fame of browning, and a teafpoonful of lemon-pickle, ftrain it, difh them up, with bread-fauce in a bafon, made the fame way as for the boiled turkey:— N.B. When a pheafant is roafted, ftick the feathers on the tail before you fend it to the table.

To roaft
young CHICKENS

WHEN you roaft young chickens, pluck them very carefully, draw them, only cut off the claws, trufs them, and put them down to a good fire, finge, duft, and bafte them with butter; they will take a quarter of an hour roafting, then froth them up, lay them on your difh, pour butter and parfley in your difh, and ferve them up hot.

69

To roaft
LARKS

PUT a dozen of larks on a fkewer, tie it to the fpit at both ends, dredge and basfte them, let them roaft ten minutes, take the crumbs of a half-pennt-loaf, with a piece of butter the fize of a walnut, put it in a toffing-pan, and fhake it over a gentle fire till they are brown, lay them betwixt your birds, and pour over them a little melted butter.

In Lancashire a roast chicken is always stuffed and served with a rich gravy, rolls of bacon and bread sauce. Pheasant with Chestnuts and Rabbit with Dumplings. I am sure you will enjoy making the following recipes, which will give you a true flavour of the north.

ROAST CHICKEN WITH PARSNIPS
(Margaret Cartmel)

1 1.8kg/4lb Roasting chicken
50g/2 oz chicken dripping
450g/1lb parsnips, peeled and quartered length-ways
4 rashers of streaky bacon (rindless)
4 large sausages, cut in half.

STUFFING

100g/4 oz fresh breadcrumbs
150ml/quarter pint of chicken stock
chicken liver, finely chopped
1 small onion, finely chopped
1 tablespoon of parsley, thyme, chives and sage mixed

1 tablespoon shredded suet
1 tablespoon ground almonds
salt
freshly milled pepper.

Wipe the chicken, remove the giblets and set aside the liver.

For the stuffing soak the breadcrumbs in the chicken stock, adding all the other ingredients after ten minutes.

Spoon the stuffing into the cavity of the chicken until the breast is quite plump, secure with a skewer.

What ever is left make into little balls and cook with the bacon rolls for the last 25 minutes of cooking.

Melt chicken dripping in the roasting tin, pre-heating the oven Gas mark 6, 400f/200c. Paste the breast and thighs of the chicken with the dripping, seasoning with salt and freshly milled pepper. Put in the roasting tin cover loosely with cooking foil.

Roast in the centre of the oven for one hour.

Make up the bacon rolls by cutting the streaky bacon in half, wrapping each piece around the 8 pieces of sausage.

Reduce the heat to gas 4, 350f/180c, remove the foil and place in the bacon rolls and parsnips around the chicken, basting well and cook for a further 35 minutes. Using the stock to make a rich gravy.

PHEASANT WITH CHESTNUTS
(Peter Smith, Newburgh)

2 Oven-ready pheasants, jointed
225g/8 oz peeled chestnuts
25g/1 oz butter
1 tablespoon vegetable oil
2 onions, skinned and sliced
45ml/3 tablespoons plain flour
450ml/three-quarters pint chicken stock
150ml/quarter pint of sherry
10ml/2 tablespoons redcurrant jelly
bouquet garni
1 orange, grated rind & juice
freshly milled pepper
salt

Into a large frying pan, place the butter and oil, heat, adding the pheasant cooking for 6 minutes. Remove the pheasant and place it into an oven-proof casserole.

Fry the chestnuts and onions for 3 minutes in the remaining oil, add to the pheasant.

Stir the flour into the fat in the pan cooking for 2 minutes.

Stir in the stock and sherry, bring to the boil, stirring until thick and smooth, seasoning to taste. Pour over the pheasant, adding the bouquet garni, redcurrant jelly and juice and rind of the orange. Cover and bake at Gas mark 4, 350f/180c for 60 minutes until tender.

Remove the bouquet garni and serve with Game Chips.

RABBIT WITH DUMPLINGS
(Rosemary Bromley)

Rabbit can be easily obtained jointed and ready for the oven, dumplings have been a northern delicacy for hundreds of years.

To make the dumplings, mix 75g/3 oz self-raising flour, with 40g shredded suet and a tablespoon of chopped chives, salt and freshly milled pepper with enough water or chicken stock to make a soft dough. 30 minutes before the end of cooking time, add the little dough balls on the top of the casserole.

225g/8 oz rindless streaky bacon
chopped 6 rabbit portions
568ml/1 pint chicken stock
2 leeks, trimmed, sliced and washed
8-10 shallots, peeled
225g/8 oz carrots, peeled and sliced
3 celery sticks, chopped
30ml/2 tablespoons Worcestershire sauce
30ml/2 tablespoons port
pinch of tarragon
salt
freshly milled pepper

Fry the bacon in large frying pan, gently for 3 minutes, add the rabbit, frying for a further 6 minutes.

Add all the rest of the ingredients except the flour and the stock, cook for a further 2 minutes add the flour and slowly add the stock.

Place into an oven proof casserole, cover and bake at Gas mark 3, 325f, 170c for 1 hour. Add the dumplings and cook for a further 35 minutes.

PIGEONS IN CIDER
(Sharon & Ben Gutcher, Burscough)

6 pigeon breasts
4 rashers rindless streaky bacon
1 onion, finely shredded
4 shallots, peeled
225g/8 oz button mushrooms
50g/2 oz raisins
300ml/half pint of cider
50ml/2 fl oz chicken stock
1 bay leaf
30ml/2 tablespoons of plain flour

Place the pigeon breast on the rashers of bacon in a oven-proof casserole. Cover with the shallots, finely shredded onion, raisins, cider and bay leaf. Leave for 24 hours. Cook in pre- heated oven at Gas 4, 350f/ 180c, for 2 hours. Add the mushrooms, cook for a further hour and thicken with flour before serving.

MARMALISED BREAST OF DUCK
To David Hall

This is the most popular dish, I have ever created. When friends come around for dinner, I am always asked for this recipe, which I created for a major food company.

4 Duck Breasts, excess fat removed and trimmed
85g/3 oz thick cut marmalade
85g/3 oz blackcurrants
225g/8 oz shallots, peeled and sliced
120ml/4 fl oz port
30ml/1 fl oz brandy

15ml/1 tablespoon rose petal vinegar
1 teaspoon pink peppercorns
freshly milled black pepper
salt
30g/1 oz unsalted butter
30ml/1 fl oz oil

Heat the oil and butter in a roasting pan, season lightly. Sear the duck breasts on the meat side over a high heat until lightly browned, turn the breasts onto the skin side and drain.

Add all the rest of the ingredients and cook in a pre-heated oven Gas 8, 230c/450f for 15 minutes, basting every 5 minutes.

Remove the duck breasts and slice each duck breast into 8 slices lengthways, keeping warm on a serving tray in the oven.

Reduce the marmalade sauce over a high heat until almost like a thick sauce consistency (reduced), then pour over the slices of duck, grill for one minute before serving.

Garnish with slices of orange and mint leaves.

MARINATED VENISON STEAKS
with BLACK CHERRIES
(Chef, John Livingston)

6 slices of venison (haunch)
6 black peppercorns (crushed)
150g/5 ozs black cherries & syrup, stoned
8 shallots, peeled and sliced
3 rashers of back bacon, rindless, and chopped
6 juniper berries, crushed
30ml/2 tablespoons port
flour
freshly chopped parsley

MARINADE

300ml/half pint red wine
6 blackpepper corns
2 shallots sliced
30ml/2 tablespoons port
30ml/2 tablespoons walnut oil
15ml/1 tablespoon tarragon vinegar

Into a large glass bowl add the marinade, mixing well. Add the venison steaks and leave overnight.

Pre-set the oven to Gas 4, 350f, 180c. Take the venison steaks from the marinade and place into a baking tray. Cover with all the ingredients . Cover and bake for 35 minutes until the steaks are tender. Thicken the stock with a little flour, sprinkle with fresh parsley and serve.

DRUNKEN DUCK
(D.Garmory, Scarisbrick New Rd, Southport)

900g/2lb boneless duck pieces
250ml/8 fl oz bitter
45ml/3 tablespoon flour
50g/2 oz butter
15ml/1 tablespoon oil
8 shallots peeled, sliced
100g/4 oz rindless streaky bacon
100g/4 oz button mushrooms
15ml/1 tablespoon, prepared English mustard
15ml/1 tablespoon of honey (end of cooking)
finely chopped parsley
10 red cherries

Season the flour with salt and freshly milled black pepper. Coat the duck pieces lightly with the seasoned flour, shaking off the excess and put the unused flour to one side.

Pre-heat the oven to Gas 4 180c/350f. Heat half the butter in a large frying pan, add the oil and fry the duck for 3 minutes.

Remove, drain of any excess fat and place in a deep casserole.

Add all the ingredients to the frying pan and simmer for 5 minutes, season to taste and spoon the mixture over the duck.
Cover and cook for 1 hour.

Remove the duck pieces, add the remaining butter and flour to the stock, bringing to the boil and simmer for 10 minutes, add a little honey, to take away the bitterness and pour over the duck pieces.

I sometimes add red cherries or apple puree, to give it a little more substance.

OLDE LANCASHIRE CHICKEN PIE
(Ron Terry, Burscough)

1.4kg/3lb Oven Roast Chicken, Cooked
225g/8 oz leeks
2 hard-boiled eggs
15ml/1 tablespoon finely chopped chives
100g/4 oz rindless bacon
25g/1 oz butter
25g/1 oz flour
salt
nutmeg
freshly milled black pepper
300ml/half pint chicken stock
150ml/quarter pint single cream
1x 450g/1 lb suet pastry (see recipe 000)
egg beaten to glaze

73

Skin the chicken, remove the flesh from the bones and cut into chunks. Clean the leeks, remove most of the green and cut them into 1-cm/ half inch slices, chop the bacon, cook in a saucepan until the bacon becomes crisp. Add the butter, cooking the leeks until soft and transparent, take the pan off the heat and blend in the flour and add the chicken stock, simmer and cook for 4 minutes, add more stock if required, then add the cream.

Pre-heat the oven to moderate Gas 5, 190c/375f.

Line a greased 20cm/8 in pie dish with the suet pastry and place the chicken pieces, bacon and quartered boiled eggs in the dish, season with salt and freshly milled black pepper and a little nutmeg, add the chives and pour over the leek sauce.

Cover, decorate and glaze the pie with the remaining suet pastry.

Bake in the oven for 35 to 40 minutes until golden brown.

ROAST GOOSE LIKE A SWAN
1789

Swan was popular over 100 years ago. I am pleased to see that they are now there to be admired, rather than cooked!

3·6-4·5kg/8-10lb goose, dressed weight
15ml/1 tablespoon flour
fresh breadcrumbs

STUFFING

2 cooking apples, peeled, cored and diced
1 large onion, peeled and diced
goose livers, finely chopped
50g/2 oz raisins
75g/3 oz fresh breadcrumbs
1 egg, beaten with a little chicken stock
a pinch of dried mint
salt
freshly milled black pepper

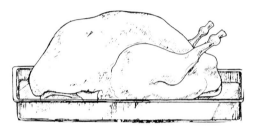

Pre-heat the oven to Gas 6, 200c, 400f. Season generously inside and out of the goose with the salt and pepper.

Make up the stuffing mixture, by blending completely the stuffing ingredients.

Stuff the goose and sprinkle lightly with the flour. Roast the goose for 20 minutes, then reduce the heat to slow cook gas 3, 170c, 325f and continue cooking for 2 hours. Prick the skin occasionally during cooking to allow the fat to escape, removing the fat from the pan several times during the cooking period. Twenty minutes before the end of cooking, sprinkle the goose with breadcrumbs, raise the oven heat again to Gas 6, 200c,400f for the final 20 minutes. I like garlic so I usually add a little garlic oil to my stuffing mixture and baste with a garlic butter, after pricking the goose.

PHEASANT IN RED WINE
(Penny Edwards, Liverpool)

1kg/2lb dressed weight (2) pheasants
10 shallots, finely chopped
200g/8 oz button mushrooms
45ml/3 tablespoons cognac
600ml/1 pint red Burgundy
300ml/half pint double cream
pheasant livers
1 garlic clove crushed
25g/1 oz butter
25g/1 oz flour
30ml/2 tablespoons olive oil
50g/2 ozs shredded ham
75g 3 oz seedless grapes
8 shallots, half cooked

Pre-heat the oven Gas 2, 150c, 300f.

Saute the pheasant into a large frying pan with the butter and olive oil, add the shallots, garlic and pheasant livers, simmer for 4 minutes.
Remove the pheasants and place them into a thick bottomed ovenproof casserole and keep them warm.

Add the wine to the frying pan, simmer for 5 minutes then add the mushrooms and simmer until the liquid is reduced by half. Thicken the sauce with the flour, simmer for 2 minutes then pour the wine over the pheasants. Cover the casserole and cook in the oven for 45 minutes. Add the double cream, warm brandy, 8 shallots, shredded ham and grapes and cook for a further 10 minutes.

Just look at this recipe for hare-pie, the amount of work that goes into this dish, shows just how dedicated Mrs Raffald was to cookery and the art work to decorate the pastry top!

A HARE-PIE
Mrs Elizabeth Raffald, 1769.

CUT a large hare in pieces, season it well with mace, nutmeg, pepper and salt, put it in a jug, with half a pound of butter, cover it close up with a paste (pastry) or cloth, set it in a copper of boiling water, and let it stew one hour and a half, then take it out to cool, and make a rich forcemeat (stuffing) of a quarter of a pound of scraped bacon, two onions, a glass of red wine, the crumb of a penny loaf, a winter savoury, the liver cut small, a little nutmeg, season it high with pepper and salt, mix it well up with the yolks of three eggs, raise the pie, and lay the forcemeat in the bottom, lay in the hare, with the gravy that came out of it, lay the lid on (pastry), and put flowers or leaves on it (pastry cut into those shapes); it will take an hour and a half to bake it — it is a handsome side-dish for a large table.

Chapter 10

MEAT DISHES

I am often asked what is the difference between shepherd's pie and cottage pie? The answer is in the name, a shepherd's pie is made with lamb and cottage pie with beef. The favourite of the north without doubt is shepherd's pie.

Put the lamb into a casserole and allow to cool. Top with the mashed potato and sprinkle with cheese. Bake in the oven for 20 minutes and serve with fresh green peas.

The flavour that comes from the cowheel, makes the meat melt in your mouth.

SHEPHERD'S PIE
(Pat Wells)

450g/1 lb lean minced lamb
1 large onion, skinned and finely chopped
2 carrots, peeled and finely diced
25g/1 oz plain flour
300ml/half pint lamb stock
15ml/1 tablespoon tomato puree
salt
freshly milled black pepper
pinch of thyme
450g/1lb creamed potatoes with milk and butter, highly seasoned.
75g/3 oz Lancashire cheese, crumbled

Pre-heat the Oven to Gas mark 6, 200c, 400f.

Dry fry the lamb in a non-stick saucepan, with the onion and diced carrots for 10 minutes. Add the flour and cook for a further 2 minutes. Blend in the stock and tomato puree, simmer for 20 minutes, seasoning with the salt, pepper and thyme.

STEAK AND COWHEEL PIE
(Carolyn Hall)

700g/1½ lb braising steak, trimmed of fat & cubed
275g/10 oz Cowheel meat, chopped
1 large onion, skinned & chopped
25g/1 oz plain flour, highly seasoned
150ml/quarter pint beef stock
150ml/quarter pint of guinness
50g/2 oz beef dripping
pinch of thyme
15ml/1 tablespoon worcestershire sauce
15ml/1 tablespoon tomato puree
salt
freshly milled black pepper
egg wash
150g/6oz Suet pastry (page 000)

Toss the steak in the seasoned flour. Melt the dripping in a large saucepan and lightly fry the onion for 3 minutes. Add the steak and cowheel and cook for 10 minutes, until lightly browned, slowly adding the stock, guinness, tomato puree, worcester sauce and thyme. Season, cover and gently simmer for 80 minutes.

Pre-heat the oven at gas 6, 200c, 400f

Spoon the mixture into a large pie dish , cover with the pastry lid, pressing lightly to seal the edges. Brush lightly with egg wash.

Make leaves with any excess pastry. Bake in the oven for 35-40 minutes.

BEEF & POTATO PIE
(Pauline Garmon-Jones)

5 large potatoes, peeled and diced into
2.5cm/1 inch cubes.
450g/1lb roughly minced beef
175g/6 oz finely chopped beef kidney
1 large onion chopped
150ml/¼ pint beef stock
salt
freshly milled black pepper
pinch of thyme
150g/6 oz suet pastry (page 000)

Pre-heat the oven at Gas 4, 180c/350f.

Place into a large casserole/pie dish all the ingredients except the pastry. Cover and cook for 2 hours.

Place the pastry lid on the pie, egg wash/ glaze, return to the oven and cook for 35 minutes at gas 6, 200c, 400f.

Serve with red cabbage, pickles and crusty bread.

LANCASHIRE POT ROAST
(Kath Thomas)

I think the Lancashire Pot roast, when served in the pot from the dining table, with beetroot and English mustard, out-shines several of the classical English dishes of the last century.

This has been in my family's recipe book for the last 5 generations. Try to use all baby vegetables where possible and the largest casserole your oven will take.

This will feed a family of eight and whatever is left will make a beautiful soup, if put into a blender with beef stock (should there be any left).

1.4kg/3lb Topside
50g/2 oz beef dripping
500g/1lb baby new potatoes
(Jersey Royal), cleaned
225g/8 oz dried haricot beans
(soaked overnight)
225g/8 oz shallots, peeled
225g/8 oz onions, peeled, quartered
225g/ 8 oz baby carrots, top, tailed
and peeled
225g/8 oz baby leeks, cleaned and sliced
225g/8 oz button mushrooms
1 small swede, peeled & sliced
thyme
1 clove crushed garlic
275ml/½ pint of beef stock
150ml/¼ pint of red wine
salt
freshly milled black pepper

Pre-heat the Oven to Gas 4, 350f, 180c.

Drain the water off the haricot beans that have been left to soak overnight.

Fry the beef in the dripping in a large frying pan, sealing and browning the meat all over. The place the meat into the centre of the large casserole, surrounded by the beans.

Lightly fry all the other vegetables and then surround the beef with them. Sprinkle the beef with thyme and garlic, season well with salt and pepper, pour over the wine and stock. Cover and cook for 90 minutes.

Serve and carve at the table.

BEEF STEW & DUMPLINGS
Lancashire Lodge — Bob Yoxall

This is the stuff that made Bob Yoxall so big. It is a regular item at The Lancashire Lodge in Wigan.

900g/2lb shin beef, trimmed, fat
removed and cubed
50g/2 oz seasoned flour
50g/2 oz beef dripping
275g/10 oz shallots, peeled
600ml/1 pint beef stock
300ml/½ pint of guinness
225g/8 oz carrots, peeled & diced
225g/8 oz potatoes, peeled & diced
225g/8 oz turnip, peeled & diced
100g/4 oz finely chopped onion
2 sticks celery, cleaned & diced
salt
freshly milled black pepper

DUMPLINGS

100g/4 oz self-raising flour
50g 2 oz shredded suet
salt
pepper
water or beef stock to mix
chopped parsley

Sieve the flour into a mixing bowl. Stir in the suet and season.

Carefully mix in just enough water to make a soft dough. You can also use beef stock and a little parsley should you wish to make into little floured dough balls and set to one side.

Season and flour the meat. Heat the dripping in a flameproof casserole or heavy based 2.3 litre/4 pint saucepan, cook the shallots and onions for 4 minutes. Add the meat and fry until lightly browned. Add the stock & stout, season and bring to the boil, removing any scum from the surface.

Add the rest of the vegetables, reduce the heat and simmer for 2 hours. 20 minutes before end of cooking time, add the dumplings.

BRAISED OXTAIL

1.1kg fresh oxtail jointed
2 onions, peeled and sliced
225g/8 oz carrots,peeled & sliced
225g/8 oz leeks, cleaned and sliced 2 sticks
celery, sliced
25g/1 oz flour
25g/1 oz beef dripping
25g/1 oz tomato puree
1 bay leaf
pinch of thyme

1.1 ltr of boiling beef stock
salt
freshly milled pepper

Pre-heat the oven to Gas 2, 300f, 150c.

Melt the dripping in a frying pan, add the oxtail and fry the oxtail for 8 minutes, turning frequently.

Place the pieces onto a large plate. Fry the vegetables until they are brown, placing them into a large casserole. Add the thyme and bay leaf, covering with beef stock.

Rub the oxtail pieces into the seasoned flour, add to the casserole, cover and cook for 3 hours.

Thicken with more flour if necessary.

Taken from *The Cook's Oracle*
by William Kitchiner MD 1827.

This Joint is said to owe its name to King Charles the Second, who dining upon a Loin of Beef, and being particularly pleased with it, asked the name of the Joint, said for its merit it should be knighted, and henceforth called Sir-Loin. The table on which he knighted the Sir Loin can still be seen at Hoghton Tower.

Our second Charles of fame facete,
On Loin of Beef did dine;
He held his sword, pleas'd, o'er the meat,
Arise thou fam'd Sir-Loin.

Ballad of the New Sir John Barleycorn.

CHEESE & PORT STEAKS
Dedicated to H.R.H. The Princess Royal

4 x 225g/8 oz Sir-loin steaks, trimmed
and seasoned
150g/6 oz Lancashire or Stilton cheese
30ml/2 tablespoons port
30ml/2 tablespoons double cream
25g/1 oz best butter, softened
50g/2 ozs crushed walnuts
1 clove garlic, crushed
freshly ground black pepper
freshly chopped parsley

Into a glass bowl, put the cheese, garlic, port, cream & butter.

Blend it all together, seasoning it well.

Put the steak onto a grill and cook from 3 to 10 minutes either side or to your liking. Place the steaks onto a baking sheet covering each steak with the cheese mixture, sprinkle with crushed walnuts and bake in a hot oven Gas 7, 425f/220c for 7 minutes.

Serve with grilled mushrooms, tomatoes and duchess potatoes.

Sprinkle with freshly chopped parsley.

CROWN OF LAMB with FRESH MINT STUFFING
(Jenny Speed, Newburgh)

2 best end necks of lamb, each with
6 cutlets, chined
12 shallots, peeled
12 baby potatoes, peeled
200g/8 oz button mushrooms

200g/8 oz baby parsnips
30g/1 oz best butter
1 onion, peeled & chopped
2 bramley's, peeled, cored & chopped
100g/4 oz fresh wholemeal breadcrumbs
30ml/2 tablespoons fresh, chopped mint
pinch of tarragon
pinch of thyme
1 egg
salt
freshly milled pepper
25g/1 oz plain flour
450ml/¾ pint of lamb stock
sprigs of fresh mint to garnish

Pre-heat the oven to Gas 4, 180c/350f.

Trim each cutlet bone to a depth of 2.5cm/1 inch. Bend the joints around, the fat side inwards, and sew together using butchers string or strong cotton to form a crown, covering the exposed bones with foil to stop them burning.

Melt the butter in a saucepan and cook the onion and apples until brown, add the breadcrumbs, tarragon, mint, thyme and egg, seasoning to taste, fill the centre of the crown with the stuffing . Place the joint into a large roasting tin, surround the crown with the potatoes, shallots and parsnips, baste with a little garlic oil, cover with foil and cook for 50-60 minutes.

Transfer the crown and the vegetables to a warm serving dish and keep warm. Add the flour to the roasting tin, cooking for 3 minutes, add the stock, blending in slowly to form a rich mint and lamb gravy. Pour through a sieve into a warm gravy boat, garnish the crown of lamb with fresh sprigs of mint, wrap small pieces of frilled foil around each lamb bone to look like a crown, or use cutlet frills and serve.

ROAST SIRLOIN OF BEEF & YORKSHIRE PUDDING

1.4kg/3 lb boned & rolled Sirloin beef
salt
freshly milled black pepper
25g/1 oz beef dripping

see Yorkshire Pudding recipe (page 000)

Pre heat the oven to Gas mark 4 , 180c/350f. Put the Sirloin on a roasting rack in a shallow roasting tin, with the thickest layer of fat uppermost. Pour over the dripping and season. Cook for 45 minutes, basting occasionally with the juices from the tin. Cover the meat with foil and place on the bottom of the oven while cooking the Yorkshires.

Increase the temperature to Gas 7, 220c/425f and cook the Yorkshire puddings for 35-40 minutes.

Serve with the sliced roast beef and a rich onion gravy made from the juices.

STEAK & KIDNEY PUD
(Gerry Halpin)

675g/1½lb Rump steak, gristle &
fat removed, cubed
225g/8 oz ox kidney, diced seasoned
flour
1 large onion, peeled and chopped
pinch of thyme
30ml/2 tablespoons worcestershire sauce
a little rich beef stock

SUET

350g/12 oz plain flour
15ml/1 tablespoon baking powder
175g/6 oz suet
salt
pepper

To make the suet crust, sift the flour, baking
powder and salt into a large bowl. Add a little
pepper and the suet. Stir in approximately 10
-12 tablespoons cold water to make a soft,
but not sticky dough.

Grease a 1 litre/one & three quarter pint
pudding bowl.

Place the dough on a floured surface and
knead it gently and lightly. Roll it out to a
round, large enough to line a bowl. Cut out a
quarter of the circle to make a lid. Using the
rest of the dough to line the buttered pudding
bowl.

Toss the steak & kidney into the seasoned
flour. And place into the lined pudding bowl
with the onions and herbs, add the gravy and
worcestershire sauce. Place on the suet crust
lid, making sure it is completely sealed. Cover
the top with a buttered sheet of greaseproof
paper, cover this with cooking foil or a cloth
and tie firmly with string.

Place the pudding in a steamer or a large pan
of water, covered and simmer for 5 hours,
checking the water does not boil dry.

When cooked, cut a small hole into the top of
the pudding and top up with a little onion
gravy.

PORK CHOPS with APPLE
Marc McCrone, Preston

4 thick pork chops, trimmed
2 large bramley apples, cored and sliced
into apple rings
30ml/2 tablespoons cooking oil
30ml/2 tablespoons brown sugar
25g/1 oz butter
60ml/4 tablespoons apple juice
15ml/1 tablespoon dry English mustard
salt
freshly milled pepper
sprig of mint
freshly chopped parsley

Pour the cooking oil into a frying pan. Season
the chops with salt and pepper and dried
English mustard, rubbing in well.

Fry over a moderately high heat for 5
minutes on each side.
While the chops are cooking toss the apple
rings into the sugar.

Then remove the chops to a warm large
serving dish. Add the butter to the pan, when
it is melted add the apple rings to the pan and
cook for 3 minutes either side until golden
brown, then return the chops to the pan and
cook for a further 5 minutes. Add the apple
juice, cook for a further 2 minutes and serve,
garnished with fresh mint and finely chopped
parsley.

CORNED BEEF HASH
for Jim O'Neil, Newburgh, 1992

Whenever I make Corned Beef Hash, for the family, I always make two, one for us and one for my good friend & neighbour Jim O'Neil.

His family, like mine, love this truly remarkable dish invented by William Kitchiner in 1817.

This is my recipe for Jim O'Neil.

675g/One half pound of cubed corned beef
25g/1 oz beef dripping
1 small finely chopped onion
8 shallots finely chopped
25g/1 oz plain flour
275ml/half pint of good beef stock
15ml/1 tablespoon Worcestershire sauce
5ml/1 teaspoon thyme
salt
freshly milled black pepper

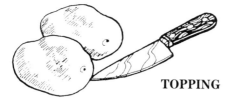

TOPPING

Blend to-gether the following ingredients

450g/1lb creamed potatoes, seasoned with
butter & milk
75g/3 oz wholemeal breadcrumbs
75g/3 oz crumbled Lancashire cheese
1 egg, blended with a little cream
salt
freshly milled black pepper

Melt the dripping in a large frying pan and cook the onion and shallots for 3 minutes. Stir in the flour, stock and worcestershire sauce, add the thyme, seasoning. Cook for a further 2 minutes. Add the corned beef and blend in slowly.

Put the mixture in an ovenproof dish and top with the potato mixture and riffle the surface with a fork. bake in the oven at Gas mark 4, 180c/350f for 30 minutes until the top is golden brown. Served with baked beans and crusty bread.

BRAISED BRISKET OF BEEF
James Edward Bridge

1.4 kg Brisket, boned & rolled
1 large onion, peeled and roughly chopped
25g/ 1 oz beef dripping
4 large tomatoes, peeled and chopped
15ml/1 tablespoon tomato puree
30ml/2 tablespoons of sherry
1 bay leaf
salt
freshly milled pepper

Pre-heat the oven to Gas 8, 230c/450f.

Heat the dripping in a large heavy frying pan, add the brisket, browning quickly all round. Place the meat with the sliced onion onto a large piece of cooking foil.

Top with the tomatoes, bay leaf, seasoning and tomato puree, seal in a neatly wrapped parcel and place in a large roasting tin and cook for 2 hours. Unwrap the meat retaining the juices in a saucepan. Combine the sherry and juices, season cook for 2 minutes, add a little flour to thicken. Serve with boiled cabbage and roast potatoes . Or it can also be served cold with a Summer Salad.

To make **BRISKET of BEEF a-la-royale**
Mrs Raffald 1769.

BONE a brifket of beef, and make holes in it with a knife, about an inch one from another, fill one hole with fat bacon, a fecond with chopped parfley, and a third with chopped oyfters, feafoned with nntmeg, pepper, and falt, till you have done the brifket over, then pour a pint of red wine boiling hot upon the beef, dredge it well with flour, fend it to the oven, and bake it three hours or better; when it comes out of the oven take off the fat, and ftrain the gravy over the beef; garnish with pickles, and ferve it up.

BARBECUED PIG
Young Woman's Companion 1811

Prepare a pig about ten weeks old as for roasting, make forcemeat of two anchovies, six sage leaves, and the liver of the pig, all chopped very small, then put them into a mortar, with the crumb of half a penny loaf, 4 ozs butter, half a teaspoonful chyan pepper, and half pint of red wine. Beat them all together to a paste put it in the pigs belly, and sew it up.

Lay your pig down at a good distance before a large brisk fire, singe it well, put into your dripping pan three bottles of red wine, and baste it well with this all the time it is roasting. When it is half done, put under the pig two penny loaves, and if you find your wine too much reduced, add more.

When your pig is near enough, take the loaves and sauce out of your dripping pan, and put to the sauce one anchovy chopped small, a bundle of sweet herbs, and half a lemon. Boil it a few minutes, then draw your pig, put a small lemon or apple in the pigs mouth, and a leaf on each side. Strain your sauce, and pour it on boiling hot. Send it up to the table garnished with barberries and sliced lemon.

BEAST'S HEART larded
Mrs Raffald 1769.

It is very interesting to note here the unusual items available to Elizabeth Raffald's kitchen and this is what she would have sold in her shop in Manchester.

TAKE a good beaft's heart, ftuff it as before, and lard it all over with little bits of bacon, duft it with flour, and cover it with paper, to keep it from being to dry, and fend it to the oven; when baked put the heart on your difh, take off the fat, and ftrain the gravy through a hair-fieve, put it in a fauce-pan, with one fpoonful of red wine, the fame of browning, and one of lemon-pickle, half an ounce of morels, one anchovy cut fmall, a little beaten mace, thicken it with flour and butter, pour it hot on your heart, and ferve it up: garnifh with barberries.

Chapter 11

PUDDINGS, PASTRIES & CAKES

There is not an area in England that as not had a little taste of the North. You can go into shops all over England today and buy Parkin, Eccles Cakes, Chorley Cakes, Oatcakes, Teacakes, Gingerbread & Crumpets. Elizabeth Raffald started the crumpet craze in the north with her 'Orange Crumpets'. We certainly have made our mark on society since then.

To make ORANGE CRUMPETS
Mrs Raffald. 1760

TAKE a pint of cream, and a pint of new milk, warm it, and put in it a little runnet*, when it is broke stir it gently, lay it on a cloth to drain all night, and then take the rinds of three oranges, boiled as for preserving in three different waters.

pound them very fine, and mix them with the curd, and eight eggs in a mortar, a little nutmeg, the juice of a lemon, or orange, and sugar to your taste, bake them in tin-pans rubbed with butter, when they are baked turn them out, and put sack and sugar. Some put slices of pressed oranges among them.

* Runnet (rennet) is the extract from a calf's stomach. Extract of rennet can still be purchased at Chemists.

For those of you who really do think Cheesecake is a 20th century recipe, here's Mrs Raffald's from 1769.

To make CHEESE-CAKES

SET a quart of new milk near the fire, with a spoonful of runnet, let the milk be blood warm when it is broke, drain the curd through a coarse cloth, now and then break the curd gently with your fingers, rub into the curd a quarter of a pound of butter, a quarter of a pound of sugar, a nutmeg and two Naples biscuits grated, the yolk, of four eggs, and the white of one egg, one ounce of almonds well beaten, with two spoonfuls of rose water, and two of sack, clean six ounces of currants very well, put them into your curd, and mix them well together.

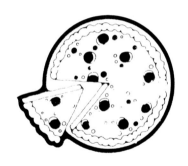

20th CENTURY LEMON CHEESECAKE

Jenny Waugh, Miry Lane, Parbold.

100g/4 oz Digestive biscuits,
crushed very fine
50g/2oz best butter
25g/1oz caster sugar
200g/7 oz full-fat soft cheese
125ml/4 fl oz soured cream
75g/3 oz caster sugar
2 eggs, separated
15g/½ oz gelatine
45ml/3 tablespoons of water
grated rind and juice of 1 large lemon

Melt the butter in a saucepan, blending in the crumbs and sugar.
Put the mixture into a 15cm/6 inch loose-bottomed cake tin, pressing the mixture to cover the base completely. Put it in the fridge to cool.

Into a clean mixing bowl, beat the sugar and cheese, then gradually add the egg yolks, beat well stirring in the soured cream.

Into a heat proof bowl put the 45ml/3 tablespoons of water, sprinkling the gelatine until it is completely dissolved. Add this to the cheese mixture with the lemon juice and rind. In another clean bowl, whisk the egg whites until stiff and peaky.

Fold carefully into the cheese mixture. Pour into the prepared tin and chill for 60 minutes. When it is set, remove from the tin very carefully onto a plate for serving.

When serving always use a warmed knife and clean it in hot water every time you slice. This will give you clean even slices of cheesecake.

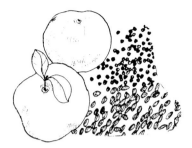

ECCLES CAKES

Eccles cakes, Banbury cakes, Coventry Godcakes, Hawshead cake and Chorley cakes all belong to the same class. They consist of pastry short or puff as the case may be, round as in case of Eccles and Chorley, the Eccles being the smaller. Each are filled with a special mixture, similar to the character of the mincemeat we put in pies at Christmas .

'When racing and fighting were all at an end,
To an ale-house each went with a sweetheart
or friend;
Some went to Shaw's, others Phillip's chose,
But me and my Moll to the Hare and Hounds
goes.

(Chorus)

With music and cakes
For to keep up the wakes
Among wenches and fine country beaux.

It is said Elizabeth Raffald gave her recipe as a wedding present to a servant who had served her well and was going to live at Eccles, and that the girl made and sold the cakes so successfully that she made her fortune.

Here is my recipe for Eccles cakes. These have been made for the Eccles 'wakes' from time immemorial:

ECCLES CAKES
(author)

225g/8 oz puff pastry
25g/1 oz best butter
100g/4 oz currants
25g/1 oz chopped mix peel
50g 2 oz demerara sugar
2.5ml/half teaspoon ground mixed spice
pinch of nutmeg
1 egg
white caster sugar

Pre-heat the oven to Gas 7, 220c/425f.

Melt the butter in a saucepan, then stir in the currants, nutmeg, spice, peel and sugar and blend them thoroughly. Roll out the pastry very thinly, then cut into rounds (use a saucer as a guide) Place a good tablespoonful of the mixture on each round.

Gather up the edges, turn over and press with a rolling pin into a flat cake. Brush with egg white and sprinkle with caster sugar.

Make 3 small diagonal cuts across the top of each.

Place on a dampened baking sheet and bake for 15 minutes, until golden brown. Sprinkle with caster sugar and serve warm or cold with butter.

BOILED RICE PUDDING
Mrs. Raffald 1789, adapted by the author

100g/4 oz Pudding rice
100g/4 oz butter
100g/4 oz sugar
200g/8 oz currants
5 egg yolks
150ml/quarter pint of single cream
1 small nutmeg, grated
grated rind of lemon.

Boil the rice in water until it is soft, then drain it. Mash it with a rolling pin in a large glass bowl or in a blender with the egg yolks, butter, sugar, nutmeg and lemon rind. Add the currants and cream and mix well. Put the mixture into a pudding basin and cover with a pudding cloth or cooking foil. Steam for 45 minutes.

MANCHESTER TART

175g/6 oz flaky pastry, rolled out
strawberry jam
275ml/half pint of fresh milk
rind of 1 lemon
50g/2 oz fresh breadcrumbs
50g/2oz butter
75g/3 oz caster sugar
2 eggs, separated
15ml/1 tablespoon of brandy
caster sugar for dredging

Pre-heat the oven at Gas 5, 190c/375f.

Line a 20cm/ 8 inch pie dish with the rolled out flaky pastry, spreading the bottom with strawberry jam.

Put the lemon rind and milk into a saucepan and bring to the boil. Remove from the heat and strain over the breadcrumbs. Leave to stand for 4 minutes, then blend in 25g/ 1 oz of the sugar, brandy, egg yolks and butter. Pour the mixture into the pastry case and bake in the oven for 40 minutes. Whisk the egg whites until they are stiff and peaky. Fold in the remaining sugar.

Spread the meringue over the top of the filling and dredge with the sugar. Bake for a further 10-12 minutes until the meringue is golden brown.

GOOSNARGH CAKES

This unique biscuit, somewhat like shortbread comes from the village of Goosnargh north-east of Preston and has been baked for Kings & Queens of England over the last two centuries.

175g/6 oz Plain flour
110g/4 oz butter
25g/1 oz caster sugar
15ml/1 tablespoon caraway seeds
5ml coriander
caster sugar for the topping

Pre-heat the oven at Gas 1, 140c/275f, then lightly grease a baking tray.

Into a large glass bowl sieve the flour, adding the caraway seeds, coriander, sugar and butter. Rub in the butter and knead it well to form a smooth paste. Roll out to 9mm (3/8th in) and cut into 5cm (2 inch) rounds.

Spread a little caster sugar evenly on top of each biscuit and press in evenly. Place onto the greased tray and leave to stand in a cool place for 90 minutes. Bake in the oven for 40 minutes and allow to cool on a wire rack.

GINGER PUDDING
1811

This is a very old recipe. It is for a pudding made without any moisture except the fat from the suet and melted sugar.

225g/8 oz sifted flour
225g/8 oz suet
225g/8 oz sugar
15ml/1 tablespoon ginger

Butter a pudding basin. Mix all the ingredients thoroughly. Put them into the basin, cover and tie it down tightly. Steam or boil for 3 hours.

ELIZA ACTON'S GINGERBREAD
1845, adapted by the author

5 eggs
450g/1lb golden syrup, warm
175g/6 oz brown sugar
450g/1lb flour
5ml/1 teaspoon cream of tartar
175g/6 oz butter, melted, warm
25g/1 oz ground ginger
2 lemons, grated

Pre-heat the oven to Gas Reg 2, 150c/300f
Beat the eggs well, add the warmed syrup gradually, beating all the time. Add the sugar in the same manner. Add the butter, which must be warmed , but not hot.

Add the ginger, cream of tartar to the flour and sift them all together. Add to the egg mixture.

Beat until bubbles appear in the batter, then add the flavouring.
Bake in a greased shallow tray in a slow oven for 35 minutes.

APPLE CRUMBLE
(Cliff Hayes, 1948)

Apples were in abundance throughout the north, so I have compiled the top 4 recipes that filled the belly's of the school children over the past 200 years.

675g/1½lb cooking apples, cored, peeled & sliced
50ml/2 oz apple juice
100g/4 oz brown sugar grated
rind of 1 lemon
75g/3 oz sultanas

CRUMBLE

150g/5 oz plain flour
75g/3 oz caster sugar
75g/3 oz best butter, softened, in small pieces
pinch of ginger

Pre-set the oven to Gas 4, 180c/350f. Butter a 1 ltr pie dish.

Into a saucepan add the brown sugar, apples, lemon rind and apple juice and cook until the apples are soft. Spoon the mixture into the pie dish, sprinkle with the sultanas.

Into a large mixing bowl, put all the crumble ingredients and rub the mixture together until the mixture resembles breadcrumbs (crumble). Scatter the mixture over the apples and press down lightly. Bake for 30 minutes until the crumble is golden brown.

APPLE DUMPLINGS

6 large bramley apples, peeled and cored
75g/3 oz brown sugar
6 cloves
pinch of cinnamon
200g/7 oz plain flour
75g/3 oz shredded suet
5ml/1 teaspoon baking powder
pinch of salt
75ml/3 fl oz water

Into a large mixing bowl, sift the flour, baking powder and salt.

Stir in the suet add the water to make a soft but not sticky dough. Divide the pastry into six portions, on a lightly floured surface, roll out each portion to around big enough to cover the apple.

Put an apple in the centre of each round, working the pastry around each apple until it almost meets the top. Fill each core hole with sugar and one clove. Dampen the edges of the pastry, working it together to seal the pastry top. Tie each dumpling either in a small well-floured pudding cloth or buttered pudding tins covered with foil.

Bring a large saucepan of water to the boil, add the dumplings and boil gently for 40 minutes, alternatively, steam or pressure cook.

MARIE'S APPLE SNOW

I have a sister, that is one year younger then me, who in all our years, we still love each other (not bad eh), I have to admit, her apple snow, is better than any one else's, because she uses half cream, half milk instead of all milk.

1kg/ 2¼ lb bramley apples, peeled, cored & sliced
rind of 1 lemon
175g/6 oz caster sugar
50ml/2 oz apple juice
2 eggs, separated
250ml/8 fl oz milk & cream
15ml/1 tablespoon calvados

Pre-heat the oven to Gas 3, 160c/325f.

Place in a saucepan the apples, lemon rind, calvados and apple juice. Cover and cook until the apples are cooked to a pulp.

Remove the lemon rind and beat the apple to a puree, adding 100g/4 oz of the caster sugar. Put the egg yolks into a clean glass bowl and beat them lightly.

Heat the milk & cream with 25g/1 oz sugar in a saucepan. Pour onto the egg yolks, then return the mixture to a clean saucepan and cook stirring all the time, do not allow the custard to boil.

Put the apple puree into buttered 1 ltr pie dish, pour the custard over and bake for 30 minutes.

In a clean, glass bowl, whisk the egg whites until stiff and peaky, fold in the remaining sugar and put on top of the custard. Return to the oven and bake until the meringue is set about 7 to 10 minutes.

MRS BRIDGE'S APPLE PIE

675g/1½ lb bramley apples, peeled, cored and sliced
100g/4 oz brown sugar
pinch of crushed cloves
15ml/1 tablespoon dark rum
Pastry (page 000)
caster sugar for dredging

Pre-set the oven to gas 6, 200c/400f. After making the pastry from page (000) , roll out the pastry on a lightly floured surface and use just over half to line a large pie dish. Place in the apples, sugar, rum and cloves, cover with the remaining pastry, seal the edges.Brush the pastry with a little milk and dredge with caster sugar. Bake for 20

minutes, then lower the temperature to gas 4, 180c/350f for a further 20 minutes until the pastry is golden brown, sprinkle with more caster sugar and serve hot with thick custard.

LANCASHIRE CHEESE SCONES
(For John Benson-Smith)

225g/8 oz self raising flour
110g/4 oz Lancashire Cheese, finely crumbled
5ml/1 teaspoon dry English mustard
25g/1 oz best butter softened
150ml/¼ pint fresh milk
pinch of salt

Pre-heat the oven to gas mark 7, 220c/425f.

Lightly grease a baking tray. Sieve together the flour, salt and dry mustard, rubbing in the softened butter until the mixture resembles fine breadcrumbs. Blend in 75g/ 3 oz of the cheese, add the milk and mix to a soft dough and knead it lightly. Roll the mixture out onto a floured board to 2.5cm/1 inch and cut into triangles. Brush the tops with milk and sprinkle with the remaining cheese. Place onto the baking sheet and cook for 20 minutes until golden brown. Serve cool with strawberry jam and clotted cream.

NOBBY'S JAM FRITTER'S

What would life be without my dad's Jam Fritters and Custard.

When I was knee high to a grasshopper, dad made these once a week for me, my brother Jim and my sister Marie. I watched the sweet batter being made, thinking one day, I will be making them myself.

4 slices of bread, buttered
strawberry jam
a little flour
oil for deep frying

BATTER

100g/4 oz plain flour
15ml/1 tablespoon vegetable oil
60ml/4 tablespoons milk
75ml/5 tablespoon cooled,
sugar water
2 egg whites
pinch salt

Put the jam quite thickly onto the buttered bread, then quarter slice the bread, lightly dip into flour.

To make the batter. Sift the flour and salt into a bowl. make a well in the centre of the flour and add the oil and milk. Work the flour from the sides very slowly, then beat well until smooth. Stir in 75ml/5 tablespoons sugar water. Leave the batter to stand for at least 1 hour.

Whisk the egg whites in a clean, grease-free bowl until stiff and peaky. Give the batter a final beating, then gently fold in the egg whites.

Put the oil for frying in a deep wide saucepan . Heat the oil until very hot 185f/360c. Coat the bread slices completely into the batter and fry for 3 minutes. Lift out the fritters very carefully with a slotted spoon and dry on absorbent kitchen paper. Keep them hot and serve with custard.

BREAD & BUTTER PUDDING

I was not the perfect schoolboy and the gentleman that can vouch for that was my teacher Mr Derek Billington. Not only was I bad at riting & rythmatic, It was my ambition to stop our Head master Mr Hall from singing another chorus of On the Road to Mandalay. I never did fulfil it ! But one thing that did full-fill me was the school bread and butter pud.

6 slices of buttered bread
25g/1 oz butter
50g/2 oz sultanas
50g/2 oz apricot jam
ground nutmeg
400ml/14 fl oz fresh milk
2 eggs
25g/
1 oz brown sugar
rind of 1 lemon

Pre-heat the oven to Gas 4, 180c/350f. Grease a 1 ltr deep pie dish. Cut the buttered bread

into small squares and arrange in alternate layers, buttered side up, spread the jam over the top and sprinkle with sultanas, sprinkling each layer with nutmeg.

Warm the milk in a saucepan, do not let it boil. Put the eggs into a bowl, add the sugar and beat slowly adding the milk.

Strain the mixture over the bread, sprinkle with nutmeg and a little more sugar. Leave to stand for 35 minutes. Finally bake for 30 minutes in the oven until the custard is set.

BAKED CUSTARD TART

250ml/8 fl oz fresh milk
2 large fresh eggs
50g/2 oz caster sugar
grated nutmeg
100g/4 oz plain flour
50g/2 oz margarine
salt
flour

Pre-heat the oven to Gas 5, 190c/375f. Line a greased sandwich tin with greaseproof paper. Sift the flour and a pinch of salt into a bowl, rub in the margarine until the mixture resembles breadcrumbs, add alittle water to make a stiff dough. Press the dough together with your finger-tips. Roll out on a lightly floured board and line the sandwich tin.

Put the milk into a saucepan and bring to just below boiling point. Put the sugar and eggs into a clean heat-resistant bowl and mix well, pour in the milk and whisk. Strain the mixture into the pastry case and sprinkle the top with nutmeg. Bake for 12 minutes, then lower the oven temperature to Gas 2, 150c/300f and bake for a further 15-20 minutes until the custard is set.

ALMOND MACAROONS

150g/5 oz caster sugar
100g/4 oz ground almonds
10ml/2 teaspoons ground rice
2 egg whites
halved glace cherries

Pre-heat the oven to Gas 3, 160c/325f. Grease a baking tray and cover with rice paper.

Whisk the egg whites in a clean, grease-free bowl until they are frothy and not stiff enough to form peaks. Stir in the sugar, ground almonds and rice. Beat with a wooden spoon. Place spoonfuls of the mixture about 5cm/2 inches apart on the rice paper, placing a halved glace cherry on each.

Bake for 20 minutes until they are a pale fawn colour. allow to cool before moving onto a wire rack to cool even more.

LANCASHIRE PARKIN

This is were the battle of the roses first started. Was Parkin originally from Yorkshire or Lancashire. It truly is a northern cake and the Lancashire recipe has more oatmeal and uses nutmeg and treacle, rather than syrup and less flour in it than the Yorkshire Parkin. The mix for Lancashire Parkin has to stand all night before baking. I have several recipes for this November 5th favourite. I am still looking to solve the battle over the origins of this favourite cake.

225g/8 oz oatmeal
50g/2 oz brown sugar
75g/3 oz plain flour
5ml/1 teaspoon ground ginger
pinch nutmeg
110g/4 oz butter
225g/8 oz black treacle or golden syrup
75ml/2 fl oz milk
pinch bicarbonate of soda
pinch of salt

Pre-heat the oven to gas 2, 150c/300f.

Into a large bowl mix the flour, oatmeal, ginger, salt, sugar, nutmeg and bicarbonate of soda.

Melt the treacle and butter in a saucepan, adding the dry ingredients then stir in the milk. Leave to stand all night.

Line a bread baking tin with grease-proof paper and pour in the mixture. Bake for 75 minutes. It is cooked when the parkin springs back when an impression is made with the finger.

BURY SIMNEL CAKE
from 1740.

This cake was always baked on Mothering Sunday, the 4th Sunday in Lent, this religious cake is the symbol of thousands of years of Christian festivals. This is just the basic recipe. The original recipes has 12 marzipan balls set around the top of the cake, representing the 12 apostles or blanched almonds in the shape of a cross, after the cake had been baked. It was then spread with apricot jam and covered with marzipan.

INGREDIENTS

Flour, butter, lard, salts of ammonia, sugar, almonds, currants, nutmeg, cinnamon, candied peel, eggs and a little milk.
The mix being very similar to Christmas cake, this is the method which would have been used to make it in 1740.
Rub the butter and lard into the flour. Pound the salts of ammonia and mix well. Then mix well all the other ingredients.
Blend them with the eggs into a stiff dough which would then have been made into the form of a batch loaf.

FLUMMERY

For this recipe you will need a double boiler or a basin which will fit into the top of a pan of boiling water.

575ml/1 pint double cream
20g/¾ oz gelatine
50g/2 oz caster sugar
15ml/1 tablespoon orange flower water
Juice & grated rind of 1 lemon.

Place all the ingredients into a double boiler or basin. Stir gently until the sugar and gelatine are completely dissolved.

Pour into small pudding tins or custard cups. Allow to cool , then place in the fridge for 2 hours.

ME MAMMY'S MALT LOAF

It was in 1986, I had only been home from London a month. I asked my mother to bake me some of her famous mince pies, It was two months off christmas, then again its christmas every day when you have tasted my mums mince pies.

The following morning my mother was there with a dozen pies and a small malt loaf. ''Let me know if you like it and I'll bake you another tomorrow, and its healthy'' she said.

125g/4 oz All Bran
125g/4 oz Sugar
175g/6 oz Sultanas and currants
200ml/7 fl oz fresh milk
175g/6 oz Self raising flour

Pre-set the Oven to Gas 3 170c/325f.

Into a large mixing bowl put the All Bran, it is important that the bran is placed on the bottom first. Add the sugar, currants and milk, allowing this to stand for one hour.

Then add the flour, blending for about 4 minutes until all the ingredients are blended thoroughly together.

Place the mixture into an oblong 3 inch deep, bread or cake tin, lined with greaseproof paper. Bake in the oven for 1 hour. Allow to cool and leave for at least 6 hours before slicing.

I prefer my malt loaf with fresh butter, it is healthier eaten without!

TANSEY-PUDDING with ALMONDS
Mrs Elizabeth Raffald 1789

This recipe gives you an insight into what products we take for granted, like greasepaper, cooking foil, measures & food colouring.

BLANCH four ounces of almonds, and beat them very fine, with rose-water, slice a French roll very thin, put on a pint of cream boiling hot, beat four eggs very well, and mix with the eggs when beaten a little sugar, and grated nutmeg, a glass of brandy, a little tansey, and the juice of spinage to make it green, put all the ingredients into a stew-pan, with a quarter of a pound of butter, and give it a gentle boil; you may either boil it or bake it in a dish, either with a crust or writing paper.

BIBLE CAKE
(dedicated to Newburgh Church)

This recipe is taken from my book *The Golden Age of Cookery*.

Television has helped the catering trade a great deal with gourmet classes and stories on our great cooks, but before television there were lots of interests in the Victorian homes and one of those interests was Bible Cake. This must be one of the most famous cake recipes and dates back before Elizabeth Raffald. If a mental picture can be formed of the rather old fashioned and clumsy equipment, perforce used by the Victorian lady's of the north, it may be surprising to find that for this recipe the cook needed a Bible — Authorised Version — and, it will be appreciated, a considerable amount of time. So if you have a Bible here i a very old recipe:

1 225g/8 oz butter = Judges V, verse 25
2 225g/8 oz sugar = Jeremiah VI, 20
3 15ml/1 tablespoon honey = 1 Samuel XIV , 25
4 3 eggs, = Jeremiah XVII, 11
5 225g/8 oz raisins = 1 Samuel XXX, 12
6 225g/8 oz figs, chopped = Nahum III, 12
7 50g/ 2 oz almonds, blanched & chopped = Numbers XVII, 8
8 450g/1 lb plain flour = 1 Kings IV, 22
9 Spices to taste = Chronicles IX
10 pinch of salt, = Leviticus II, 13
11 5ml/1 tspoon leaven baking powder = Amos IV, 5
12 45ml/3 tablespoon milk = Judges IV, 19

Pre-heat the oven to Gas 3, 160c/325f.

Beat Nos 1, 2 and 3 to a cream; add 4, one at a time beating vigorously. Beat again Nos 5,6 and 7 adding 8, 9, 10 and 11 blend them into the mixture with no 12.

Put the mixture into a large greased and lined baking tin and bake for 90 minutes.

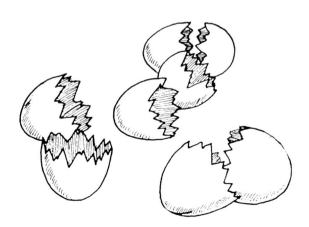

Chapter 12

PRESERVES
(HOME-MADE JAMS & JELLIES)

Observations on PRESERVING
Elizabeth Raffald 1789

WHEN you make any kind of jelly, take care you do not let any of the seeds from the fruit fall into your jelly, nor squeeze it too near, for that will prevent your jelly from being clear; pound your sugar, and let it dissolve in the syrup before you set it on the fire, it makes the scum rise well, and the jelly a better colour: it is a great fault to boil any kind of jellies too high, it makes them of a dark colour; you must never keep green sweet-meats in the first syrup longer than the receipt directs, lest you spoil their colour; you must take the same care with oranges and lemons; as to cherries, damsons, and most sort of stone- fruit, put over them either mutton-suet, rendered, or a board to keep them down, or they will rise out of the syrup and spoil the whole jar, by giving them a sour bad taste; observe to keep all wet sweet-meats in a dry cool place, for a wet damp place will make them mould, and a hot place will dry up the virtue, and make them candy; the best direction I can give, is to dip writing paper in brandy, and lay it close to your sweet-meats, tie them well down with white paper, and two folds of thick cap-paper to keep out the air for nothing can be greater fault than bad tying down, and leaving the pots open.

Author's Note: This is so true, today we have preserving jars and screw top jars, which are sealed with pressure rings and the basics are Mrs Raffalds observations. Here is her recipe for Red Currant Jelly with my modern method.

To make REDCURRANT JELLY
Mrs Raffald 1789

GATHER your currants when they are dry and full-ripe, strip them off the stalks, put them in a large stew-pot, tie the paper over them, and let them stand an hour in a cool oven, strain them through a cloth, and to every quart of juice add a pound and half of loaf sugar, broken in small lumps, stir it gently over a clear fire till your sugar is melted, skim it well, let it boil pretty quick twenty minutes, pour it hot into your pots; if you let it stand it will break the jelly, it will not set so well when it is hot; put brandy-papers over them, and keep them in a dry place for use.

N.B. You may make a half red and half white currants of the same way.

REDCURRANT JELLY
(Jim Hamer, Doffcocker)

For this recipe you will need a jelly bag which can be obtained from most major stores.

1.4kg/3lb redcurrants
sugar
45ml/3 tablespoons port
15ml/1 tablespoon brandy

Remove the currants from their stalks. Put the currants in a preserving pan with 568ml/1 pint water and simmer gently for 25 minutes, until the fruit is pulpy and soft, stirring to prevent sticking. Spoon the fruit pulp into a jelly bag or cloth attached to the legs of an upturned stool or an object similar to, and leave to strain into a large clean bowl for 1 day. DO NOT SQUEEZE.

Discard the pulp remaining in the jelly bag.Measure the extract and return it to the pan with 450g/1lb of sugar to each 568ml/1 pint of extract.

Gently heat, stirring until the sugar has completely dissolved, then rapidly boil for 15 minutes, when setting point is reached, remove the pan from the heat.

Stir in the Brandy & Port, skim the surface with a slotted spoon and pot in air tight jars, cover with a little round of paper and seal.

To make BLACKCURRANT JAM
Mrs Raffald 1789.

GET your blackcurrants when they are full ripe, pick them clear from the stalks, and bruise them in a bowl with a wooden-mallet, to every two pounds of currants put a pound and a half of loaf- sugar beat fine, put them into a preserving pan, boil them full half an hour, skim it and stir it all the time, then put it in pots and keep it for use.

BLACKBERRY & APPLE JAM
(Nicola Walton)

1.8kg/4lb Blackberries
900g/2lb Bramley apples, peeled, cored and sliced
2.7kg/6lb sugar
a knob of butter

Remove any stalks from the blackberries, put them into a large saucepan with 150ml/ 1/4 pint water simmering gently until the fruit is soft and pulpy.

Put the apples in a separate pan with 150ml/ ¼ pint of water and simmer until soft, mash to a pulp with a potato masher. Add the blackberries and sugar to the apple, cook and stir until the sugar has dissolved, adding the knob of butter, simmer for 2 minutes then bring to the boil rapidly, stirring for about 12 minutes. Test for set, when setting point is reached, remove the pan from the heat and skim the surface with a slotted spoon and pot and cover.

STRAWBERRY JAM

2.7kg/6lb Strawberries
2.7kg/6lb Sugar
Juice of 2 lemons

Remove the stalks from the strawberries and rinse them in a colander under cold water for 3 minutes, let them drain for 15 minutes.

Place them into a large preserving pan with the lemon juice.

Measure the sugar into a large oven proof dish and place a pre- heated oven Gas 1/4, 110c/225f for 10 minutes.

Cook the strawberries over a low heat for 15-20 minutes, until they are tender. Take off the heat and add the warm sugar, stirring continuously until the sugar is dissolved completely.

Bring the strawberries to the boil and cook rapidly for 15 minutes until they are setting, remove any scum with a slotted spoon. Allow the jam to cool until a skin forms, then stir for a few minutes. Pot in clean jars and seal.

LEMON CURD

2 lemons, juice and rind
3 large fresh eggs
100g/4 oz best butter
200g/8 oz sugar

Beat the eggs in a clean heat -resistant bowl, mix in the juice and rind of the lemons, butter and sugar. Place over a pan of boiling water. Heat gently, stirring occasionally until the sugar has dissolved and the curd thickens about 12 minutes. Then pour into a clean dry jar , cover and seal.

PICKLED BEETROOT

1.4kg/3lb uncooked beetroot
600ml/1 pint spiced vinegar

Wash the beetroot very carefully without damaging the skins. Cook them in a large saucepan in lightly salted water until tender.

Let them stand for about 3 hours, then peel and slice them. Pack into clean jars and cover with cold spiced vinegar.

MARBLED PICKLED EGGS

At one time no matter what pub you went into in the north, you would find jars of pickled eggs, they are very rare today. They are great with salads and when you are having a snack when friends call round. I like to use quail eggs, after boiling them, I crack the shells gently and place them in cold tea. The tea stains the egg where the cracks are in the shells, giving them a marbled affect.

12 Fresh hard boiled eggs (10 minutes)
White vinegar
12 pink peppercorns
a long sprig of tarragon
2 blades of mace

After boiling the eggs for 10 minutes, plunge them into cold water to prevent a black ring forming around the yolks. When the shells are cool, either do what I did with the cold tea or shell them carefully.

Into a large clean glass jar or stone jar put the sprig of tarragon and twelve peppercorns. Pack the eggs loosely into th jar, covering with the vinegar, adding the blades of mace. Seal at once and keep for one month before opening.

To preserve GRAPES IN BRANDY
Mrs Raffald 1789.

Take some close bunches of grapes, but not too ripe, either red or white, put them into a jar, with a quarter of a pound of sugar candy, and fill the jar with common brandy, tie it close with a bladder, and set them in a dry place. Morello cherries are done the same way.

To make APRICOT-MARMALADE
Mrs Raffald 1789.

WHEN you preserve your apricots, pick out all the bad ones, and those that are too ripe for keeping, boil them in the syrup till they will mash, then beat them with a marble -mortar to a paste; take half their weight of loaf sugar, and put as much water to it as will dissolve it, boil and skim it well, boil them till they look clear, and the syrup thick like a fine jelly, then put it into your sweet-meat glasses, and keep them for use.

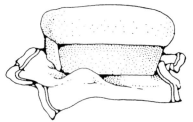

Chapter 13

A NORTHERN FESTIVE FEAST

Christmas with my family is always something special to me. When working as a full-time chef, I very rarely had christmas at home, I was to busy making everybody else's christmas dinner. With all my many years making christmas happy for thousands of people around the world, here is my recipe for a successful family Christmas.

The Victorian Christmas was very much a family affair, where dressing the table, decorating the home and christmas eve celebrations were all a magnificent part of the festive atmosphere. With a mixture of old and new I will attempt to create Christmas past & present with a setting worthy of a northern celebration.

The Christmas Cake, Mincemeat and Plum Pudding should be prepared at least six weeks before christmas.

Buy everything else you need two days before christmas and always prepare most of the food during the day of christmas eve, then you can enjoy most of the festivities.

CHRISTMAS CAKE
(1840) Twelfth Cake: Dedicated to Rev Alan Smith, Emmanuel Church, Ormskirk.

INGREDIENTS

225g/8 oz self-raising flour
225g/8 oz molasses sugar
75g/3 oz almonds, roasted, chopped
450g/1lb seedless raisins
75g/3 oz sultanas
75g/3 oz currants
75g/3 oz stoned prunes, chopped
75g/3 oz glaze cherries, halved
75g/3 oz lemon
candied peel
100ml/4 fl oz cognac
50ml/2 fl oz dark rum
50ml/2 fl oz port
5ml/1 tsp ground ginger
10ml/ 2 tsp ground cinnamon
5ml/ 1 tsp ginger 225g/8 oz best butter
75ml/3 fl oz water
4 eggs beaten

Pre-heat the oven to Gas 2, 150c/300f. Grease and line a large cake tin with greased greaseproof paper. Cream the butter with the sugar. Beat the eggs in very slowly, fold in the flour and dried fruits & spices, add the brandy, port and rum. Let this mixture stand for at least six hours.

Spoon the mixture into the prepared baking tin, level the top and bake the cake in the centre of the oven for 2 hours, then reduce the heat to Gas 1/2, 120c/250f and bake for a further 2 hours. When cool and stood for at least 3 hours, wrap the cake in tin foil and store until a week before christmas. Then top the cake with apricot jam, roll out 800g/ 2lb almond paste and cover the cake completely. Then make up 800g/ 2lb Royal Icing and decorate to your own theme.

PLUM PUDDING or CHRISTMAS PUDDING
(Nicole Cauverien)

To bring good fortune, every member of the family must stir the pudding and make a wish. Then add a silver coin, I always boil mine in salt water to make sure it is clean and wrap it in foil before adding it to the mixture. Who ever gets the portion with the coin, receives good luck throughout the following year. You must tell the family about the coin to avoid the dangers of swallowing it.

75g/3 oz plain flour
75g/3 oz shredded beef suet
75g/3 oz fresh breadcrumbs
75g/3 oz brown sugar
175g/6 oz sultanas
175g/6 oz raisins
175g/6 oz currants
25g/1 oz mixed peel, chopped
25g /1 oz chopped almonds
1 eating apple, grated
grated rind and juice of 1 lemon
grated rind and juice of 1 orange

10ml/2 tablespoons treacle
65ml/2½ fl oz sherry
30ml/2 tbsp brandy
2.5ml/½ tsp ground cinnamon
2.5ml/½ tsp grated nutmeg
2.5ml/½ tsp ground mixed spice

Grease a 1.1 litre/2 pint ovenproof pudding basin.

Mix all the ingredients together in a large mixing bowl, letting all the members of the family have a stir. Cover and leave it to stand for 24 hours in the refridgerator.

Spoon the mixture into the prepared basin, add the silver coin (if you wish to), cover with pleated greaseproof paper and cooking foil, securing it well with butchers string.

Steam for 6 hours. Allow it to cool, then remove the covers. Take it our of the basin by turning it out slowly. Recover it with greaseproof paper, foil it and store it away in a cool place until christmas.

Then when you require it steam it for 2 hours.

Turn it out onto a warmed heat-proof serving plate. Pour over some warmed brandy and ignite with a lighted wax taper. Serve with rum butter or fresh double cream.

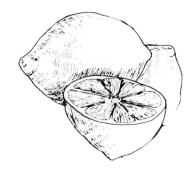

My Grandmothers Mincemeat
1899

This is my grandmother's recipe, which was passed onto me by my mother, who is the best mince pie making in Great Britain, she does not make two trays of twelve like normal people she makes ten trays for all the family to take home. Dad's daily meals then consist of nothing but mince pies to follow.

100g/4 oz shredded suet (Atora)
100g/4 oz shredded apple
225g/8 oz seedless raisins
225g/8 oz sultanas
225g/8 oz currants
50g/2 oz chopped almonds
50g/2 oz stem ginger, finely grated
50g/2 oz glace cherries, quartered
50g/2 oz mixed peel, finely chopped
175g/6 oz dark brown sugar
juice & grated rind of 1 lemon
2.5ml/½ tsp each of nutmeg, ginger
& cinnamon.
150ml/¼ pint of dark rum

Place all the above ingredients into a large bowl and mix thoroughly, cover tightly and leave to stand for 4 days for all the flavour to blend. Stir every day for the four days.

After 4 days mix thoroughly. Then spoon into large air tight jars. Sealing and leave to mature until christmas. The using my mothers pastry recipe on page 26, make the mince pies.

CHRISTMAS DINNER

There is one christmas that stands out more than any other. That was 1957 when my father was working for a company called Parker's Transport in Bolton. He was making a delivery of something to a farm on the outskirts, when the farmer asked my dad for some cinder's to fill the holes on the entrance to the farm. For this favour my dad could pick a goose for Christmas, it was a cold October and the thought of a goose for christmas, put a smile on my father's face, the farmer duly marked the goose, my dad delivered the cinders and we got a fresh goose for Christmas.

I remember plucking it with my dad on the kitchen table in York Street, Bolton. The feeling of excitement in my heart in watching the most luxurious Christmas bird of all, being plucked and cooked at the age of eight years old is something I will never forget.

ROAST GOOSE
(York Street, Bolton, 1957).

1 X 5.45 kg/12 lb Goose, dressed for cooking
900g/2 lb Bramley apples, cored, peeled
& quartered
1 large onion, peeled and chopped
15ml/1 tbsp crushed juniper berries
15ml/ 1 tbsp of sherry
salt
freshly milled black pepper

Pre-heat the oven to Gas mark 4, 180c/ 350f.

Cut the neck off close to the breast and wipe the interior cavity, trimming off any excess fat.

Into a mixing bowl add all the ingredients, blending them all together. Stuff the goose with the mixture, sew up the cavity, and put the bird, breast down, on a rack in the oven, over a dripping tray, pour 150ml/ 1/4 pint of boiling chicken stock over the bird and into the tray. Cook for 45 minutes, then turn the goose, breast up, lightly pricking it with a meat fork (not touching the flesh), to let the fat run. Cook for a further 2 and half hours, pouring out the goose fat every 15 minutes, basting the bird before you do so.

Saving the goose fat for the roast potatoes and parsnips.

103

Remove the apple mixture from the cavity of the bird, mash it with a little hot apple juice, serve this in a separate sauce boat with the roast goose.

ROAST TURKEY with TRADITIONAL BREAD SAUCE

Turkey became fashionable around 1851, when it was replaced by roast goose or roast swan, which was the tradition of the Royals Christmas menu. The northerners could only afford a chicken or a joint of beef. Some people did not even have the facilities to roast a bird or joint of beef. It was a common sight on Christmas morning to see queues outside places like Mrs Raffalds shop, using her ovens for roasting on payment of a small sum of money. The tradition of bread sauce speaks for itself, it was cheap to make and originated from the north., Which you can see from Elizabeth Raffald's recipe.!.

ROAST TURKEY
(Walter & Dot, The Windmill, Parbold)

5.45kg/12lb Fresh Hen Turkey, Oven Ready
Stuffing
450g/1lb chipolata sausages
225g/8 oz streaky bacon, rindless bacon
salt freshly milled pepper
25g/1 oz goose fat or beef dripping

Pre-heat the oven to Gas 6, 200c/400f.

Wipe the bird inside and out; reserving the giblets to make a stock for the gravy. Stuff the turkey with the stuffing. Truss the bird with butchers string. Put the bird into a large roasting tin. Rub in the goose fat or dripping, season well with salt and freshly milled pepper. Cover with cooking foil and cook for 2 hours, basting the bird every 20 minutes, turning the roasting tin around every time. Reduce the temperature to Gas 2, 150c/300f and cook for a further 2 hours, basting again every 20 minutes.

Remove the foil for the last half hour and place in the bacon, chipolata rolls.

To test whether the bird is cooked, insert a meat fork or meat skewer into the thickest part of the thigh, if the juices run clear the bird is cooked. If the juices are pink, return the bird to the oven and continue cooking until the juices run clear.

Use the juices to make a rich gravy, by adding a little port and flour to thicken the gravy, check the seasoning.

Put the turkey on a warm serving plate, surround with bacon rolls and garnish with stuffing balls and watercress.

to make SAUCE for a TURKEY
Mrs Raffald, Manchester 1777

CUT the crust off a penny-loaf, cut the rest in thin slices, put in cold water, with a few peppercorns, a little salt and onion, boil it till the bread is quite soft, then beat it well, put in a quarter of a pound of butter, two spoonfuls of thick cream, and put into a bason.

Just look how it as transformed since then. It really does annoy me to hear that bread sauce was a french invention.

TOM BRIDGE'S BREAD SAUCE

(For Norman Thomas, BBC North West)

100g/4 oz fresh breadcrumbs (white)
50g/2 oz best butter
30ml/2 tbsp double cream
1 large onion, studded with cloves
600ml/1 pint of fresh milk
1 bay leaf
6 peppercorns
salt
freshly milled pepper

Place the onion studded with cloves into a large sauce pan with the milk, peppercorns and bay leaf, add a little salt and bring to boiling point. Remove the pan from the heat and leave in a warm place to infuse for 3 hours.

Remove the onion, peppercorns and bay leaf, setting to one side for later.

Stir into the milk the breadcrumbs, adding 25g/ 1 oz butter, simmer for 12 minutes, stirring occasionally. Replace the onion and cloves until the sauce is required.

Just before serving remove the onion and peppercorns, reheating the sauce gently, blend in the remaining butter and the double cream, season to taste.

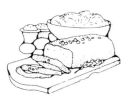

ROAST PORK WITH ORANGE

1.4kg/3 lb Shoulder of Pork, boned & rolled, rind removed.
600ml/1 pint boiling beef stock & Orange juice
25g/1 oz butter
25g/1 oz seasoned butter
2 large bramley's cored, peeled and sliced
2 onions, peeled and sliced
3 large Oranges

Pre-heat the oven to Gas mark 2 , 150c/300f.

The rind should be removed and kept for later, when you can salt it and cook in a hot oven Gas 6, 200c/400f for 1 hour until crisp. Break it into small pieces and serve it with the pork.

In a large frying pan melt the butter and fry the onion for 3 minutes, add the apple and fry for a further 3 minutes.

Lift the onion and apple out of the pan with a draining spoon, placing it into a large casserole with a lid.

Coat the pork shoulder with the seasoned flour. Increase the heat and fry the meat all over until golden brown.

While the pork is browning slice one orange and arrange the slices on the bottom of the casserole. Lift out the pork and place onto the orange slices. Roughly peel the rind of the other two oranges and scatter over the pork. Pour over the stock, cover the casserole with the lid and cook for 3 hours.

Place onto a hot serving dish with the apple onion and slices of orange, scattered with pork crackling.

SUPREME OF SALMON IN CHAMPAGNE with WILD MUSHROOMS

Dedicated to Paula & Bob Yoxall for bringing together myself and my beautiful wife Jayne. Thank You.

This is one of the specials I always make for the festive season, should anyone not like meat. Wild mushrooms and Rose Petal vinegar can very be obtained from all major supermarkets or should they not have them in stock, then from Kevin at London Larder, Manchester, telephone 061-832-9199.

6 x 225g/8 oz boned supremes
of fresh salmon
140ml/¼ pint champagne
600ml/1 pint fish stock
30ml/2 tbsp Rose Petal vinegar
140ml/¼ pint of double cream,
lightly whipped
clarified butter (recipe page 000)
170g/6 oz cold butter, diced
450g/1lb wild mushrooms, morels, ceps
& chanterelles.
5ml/ 1 tsp pink peppercorns
salt
freshly milled black pepper

Gently poach the salmon supremes in the stock, vinegar and champagne for 5 minutes. Lift the salmon out of the liquid very carefully, placing them on an oblong serving dish.

Heat the clarified butter in a large frying pan, adding the pink peppercorns and wild mushrooms cook for 3 minutes and garnish around the salmon supremes.

Reduce the fish stock over a very high heat until it reduces by a third, remove from the heat and add the diced butter, stirring in the cream. Coat the salmon with the sauce and place in a warm oven for 4 minutes. Place under a hot grill for 30 seconds before serving. Garnish with rose petals and lemon slices.

ROAST POTATOES & PARSNIPS

900g/2 lb Parsnips, peeled and
quartered lengthways
900g/2 lb Potatoes
seasoning

Pre-heat the oven to Gas 6/ 200c 400f.

Place the potatoes into a large pan and parboil them in salted water for 10 minutes then drain.

Parboil the parsnips for 3 minutes.

Place goose fat or 100g/4 oz beef dripping into a large roasting tin, place it on a direct heat to allow the fat to melt. When it is really hot, add the parsnips and potatoes, basting the vegetables with the hot fat. The place the roasting tin in the oven and cook until they are cooked about 35-45 minutes.

Drain free from the fat and serve with brussels sprouts.

OLD ENGLISH SHERRY TRIFLE
Original recipe

This is the favourite of young and old. Going back in time to the eighteenth century. There are many versions, I still prefer the original Victorian recipe which was given to me by the late Michael Smith, who's work behind the scenes in The Duchess of Duke Street, Pebble Mill at One and Upstairs, Downstairs made him very popular. He was without doubt one of the finest historians on English cookery I have ever had the pleasure of meeting. It is to Michael I would like to dedicate and finish this last recipe and my book. A truly British Institution.

The topping used for an old English trifle was always a Syllabub, from which knowledge I gained from my good friend and co-author of *A Regency Eccentric*, Colin Cooper-English.

100g/4 oz. Macaroons (see recipe 000)
45ml/3 tablespoons brandy
150ml/¼ pint white wine
45ml/3 tablespoons strawberry jam
600ml/1 pint single cream
2 fresh eggs, beaten 25g/1 oz. caster sugar

Arrange the macaroons on the bottom of a large glass trifle bowl.

Pour over the brandy and as much wine as will soak up the macaroons. Spoon over the warm jam covering completely the macaroons. Put the cream into a saucepan and bring to almost boiling point, blending in the eggs in a heat-proof mixing bowl mixing over a double saucepan or place it into a pan of boiling water, taking care it does not cover it.

Keep it simmering, stirring the custard until it thickens. Remove the saucepan from the heat and blend in the sugar, stirring until it dissolves. set this aside.

When it is nearly cold pour the custard over the macaroons and let it set overnight.

THE TOPPING FOR THE TRIFLE
SYLLABUBS
By kind permission of
Colin Cooper English.

Though there are many spellings of this word (this one becoming common after 1700), they are all derived from the earlier form — sillibouk. This was a combination of silly, meaning merry and happy, and bouk, an old dialect word for belly, also a milk pail, pitcher or pot. (Bouk has become the modern word bucket.) A Derbyshire variant of this same dish is merribouk — merry, meaning happy, plus bouk, Bub is a very old slang term for a drink, as in 'our bub and our grub'. There is also a record of a silly-bub, meaning 'buttermilk mixed with newly milked sweet milk'.

Syllabub was popular in the sixteenth and seventeenth centuries and was mostly made from cider; it was the normal refreshment on a farm in late summer during harvest-time. However, there is a strong possibility that the actual practice of blending wine and milk into a drink was carried out several thousand years ago. The following two quotations (in close proximity) are from the Bible:

I have come into my garden, my sister, my spouse; I have gathered my myrrh with my spice; I have eaten my honeycomb with my honey; I have drunk my wine with my milk: eat, O friends; drink, yea, drink abundantly, O beloved.
(Solomon's Song, Chapter 5, verse 1)

Ho, every one that thirsteth, come ye to the waters, and he that hath no money; come ye buy, and eat; yea, come, buy wine and milk without money and without price.
(Isaiah, Chapter 55, Verse 1)

The modern syllabub dates from the late seventeenth and eighteenth centuries when whipped cream replaced the milk and the syllabub became more solid — much more as we know it today.

Fruit syllabubs are very similar to fools but have the additional ingredients of wine. They are particularly pleasant in summer. All syllabubs should be served chilled and accompanied by sweet biscuits.

THE TOPPING
Banana Syllabub
(Colin Cooper English)

4 large bananas
Juice of half a lemon
600 ml/1 pint double cream
50g/2 oz caster sugar
30ml/2 tbsp white wine

TO DECORATE

Thinly sliced rind of 1 lemon.

Peel the bananas and mash them to a pulp or liquidise them with lemon juice. Place into a glass , grease-free, clean bowl the banana pulp, together with the cream, sugar and wine, beat until it starts to thicken. Pipe around the trifle and chill for 2 hours. Decorate with thinly sliced lemon rind.

To make a SYLLABUB under the COW
Mrs Elizabeth Raffald 1789

PUT a bottle of ftrong-beer and a pint of cyder into a punch bowl, grate in a fmall nutmeg, and fweeten it to your tafte; then milk as much milk from the cow as will make a ftrong froth, and the ale look clear, let it ftand an hour, and ftrew over it a few currants, well wafhed, picked and plumped before the fire, and fend to the table.

N.B. I do hope you have enjoyed reading *The History of Lancashire Cookery*, I look forward to meeting you in my next history section, *The History of Yorkshire Cookery*.

T.B.

Ninety-nine ways of Cooking and Serving Dainty Dishes of U.C.P. Tripe and Cowheel

U.C.P. Tripe and Cowheels are sold Pure and Fresh—they are always fully cooked and ready for immediate consumption cold—when used in hot dishes, they only require heating and not further cooking.

Honeycomb Tripe is best for hot dishes.

A FAMOUS FOOD

SINCE food is the very foundation of life, it is no wonder that it is the subject of so many prejudices, strange, unthinkable to us, which time and knowledge have overcome. Scarlet runners were first grown for their flowers ; tomatoes had to fight their way to favour.

Tripe has had a remarkable history from the time of the Roman Empire until its renewed prosperity under the United Cattle Products Ltd. The Romans set great store by it ; Tripe was a delicacy that graced the feasts of nobles. All through English history from Chaucer and Shakespeare down to Lamb, Burns, and Dickens, Tripe has received the meed of honourable praise from the chief wits and writers of England. It has played an important part in the diet of democracy.

Any Pecksniffian prejudice arose through misuse of the word itself, or because tripe was sold in a careless unhygienic fashion.

That was the situation which the U.C.P. found, and overcame by one of the most interesting movements in the history of food. Factories were built by U.C.P. in which every ideal of hygiene was realised. Lilywhite as a model dairy, exploiting every invention of science to maintain purity, each factory prepared and cooked Tripe which has resuscitated its ancient fame. Hundreds of shops were put into commission, superintended and given delivery of Tripe every morning, as fresh as the dawn, drawn by a fleet of eighty motor vans.

But what the public wanted above all was a *guarantee* of purity. Since one cannot brand the tripe itself, the shops were branded. The Oval Red U.C.P. Shop Window Sign is now universally regarded by the housewife as the guarantee that there U.C.P. Tripe is sold—Tripe of unchallenged delicacy and purity.

The result has been wonderful. The prestige of Tripe has gone up by leaps and bounds. The recipes of our mothers and grandmothers were unearthed, new recipes invented—295,000 copies of the previous issues of U.C.P. Recipe Book were eagerly caught up—and tripe has found its way to tables which never knew it before.

A food rich in nutriment and body-building qualities, the most digestible possible, food that is peculiarly suitable as a base for the most delicately appetising dishes, has again relieved the monotony of the English meal—the ox, the sheep, the pig.

Not only in the home where the housewife studies thrift, but in the Restaurant and Hotel as well, Tripe has made new conquests.

Tripe has been saved for the national diet. That is very important, for Tripe is a cheap food (9d. per lb.) ; but it is also a splendid food for the sedentary brain worker, for the invalid, the child, and the nursing mother. While, with its aid, the working man is given a meal tasty and satisfying, economical and strength giving.

To-day everybody studies food values. Tripe contains a fair amount of protein material, and beside fat, the following essences are contained in Tripe :— Creatinin, the basic substance of meat juice ; Glycogen, animal starch ; Sarolactic, a milky substance. This proves Tripe to be, among all solid animal foods, one of the most body-building, nutritious, and easily digested. As Miss Florence B. Jack—the cookery editor of "Good Housekeeping"—says, " it compares favourably with the rich man's oyster."

Tripe as supplied by the U.C.P. is, of course, ready for eating. Eaten cold with salad and with plenty of condiments, it forms a delicious dish. In its natural state Tripe is covered with an impervious skin which keeps the white kernel, as it were, quite untainted. The removal of this sheath requires delicate processes of scalding and washing. The tenderness of the Tripe is achieved by hours of judicious boiling. All this work is done by the U.C.P. in spotless manner and ever-flowing streams of purest water.

This edition of Recipes contains many new suggestions—295,000 copies of previous editions were so eagerly obsorbed by housewives that the U.C.P. are confident that it will act as an inspiration to the housewife to invent dishes for herself. One or two guiding points may be given.

First, be most generous with pepper and salt, and vinegar, especially salt. secondly, if you are serving hot Tripe, let it be really hot. Earthenware casseroles are ideal for Tripe.

Thirdly, Tripe makes the perfect accompaniment to tasty and piquant foods. Cheese and Bacon go well with it. Tripe used half and half with ordinary meat and vegetables makes an exquisite Irish Stew. Onions, tomatoes and celery are good companions for those hot savoury dishes welcomed by the tired husband for his evening meal.

Remember also that Calves' Feet Jelly, so highly recommended for invalids, is made from Cowheel. Cowheels are delicious for stews and soups, and with meat make exquisite pies.

Everybody knows that Tripe and Cowheels are foods of outstanding nourishing value and purity. Prejudice has been replaced by Prestige. U.C.P. Tripe has been demonstrated to be fit for a king—a right delicious food for all classes—rich and poor.

To all housewives upon whose ingenuity in the kitchen so much of home happiness depends, this little book of Recipes is dedicated.

Soups

Tripe and Tomato Soup

1 lb. Tripe.	1 oz. Dripping or Butter.
3 Onions.	1 oz. Flour.
1 lb. Tomatoes.	½ pt. Hot Milk.
1 Carrot.	A few Parsley Stalks.
Water.	Seasoning.

Well cover the trifle with cold water and bring to the boil. Add the onions and tomatoes cut in slices, and the carrot grated, a few parsley stalks and a little salt. Simmer all slowly until thoroughly cooked. Then remove the tripe and rub the soup through a sieve or colander. Rinse out the saucepan, put in the butter or dripping to melt and add the flour. Mix these together and pour on the sieved soup. Stir until boiling, add the tripe cut in small pieces and seasoning. Pour in the hot milk, and if too thick add a little more water or milk.

Cowheel and Lentil Soup

½ a Cowheel.	1 large Onion.
½ lb. Lentils.	1 Meat Cube.
1½ pts. Water.	1 tea sp. Flour.
1 Stick of Celery.	Pepper and Salt.
1 Tomato.	

Boil the cowheel in the water for one hour then remove the meat. Wash the lentils and cook them gently in the liquor until quite soft. Choose a stick of celery with green top and cut it in small pieces, removing the seeds. Grate or chop the onions finely, and cut the meat cube in pieces. Then add all to the liquor and lentils. Simmer gently for another hour. Add the flour mixed to a smooth paste with a little water, and stir until it thickens. Lastly add seasoning and serve hot. The meat from the cowheel may either be cut in small pieces and served in the soup, or served separately on steak.

Mock Turtle Soup

1 Cowheel.	1 Orange.
2 qrts. Meat Boilings.	1 oz. Flour.
2 Onions.	1 oz. Dripping.
1 Carrot.	Seasoning.
A bunch of Herbs.	A Ham Bone.

Cut the cowheel in four pieces and put it into a large saucepan with the meat boilings or any light stock, add salt and bring slowly to the boil. Skin if necessary, add the vegetables cut in pieces, a small bunch of herbs, a small ham bone or ham trimmings, and the thinly peeled rind of the orange. Simmer all slowly until the meat comes away easily from the bones, adding a little water if the liquid reduces too much. Strain when ready, remove all fat from the top of the stock, and cut the flesh in small pieces. Melt the dripping in a saucepan, when smoking hot put in the flour and let it brown slightly. Then pour in the stock and stir until boiling. Remove any scum that rises, and add more seasoning if necessary. Add also the pieces of cowheel, and the strained juice of ½ the orange.
NOTE.—A glass of port wine and a few force-meat balls may be added before serving.

Honeycomb Soup

1 lb. Honeycomb Tripe.	3 ozs. Celery.
2 ozs. Margarine.	2 ozs. Flour.
3 ozs. Chopped Onion.	3 pts. Water.
½ lb. Potatoes.	½ pt. Milk.
½ Pepper and Salt.	A small bunch of
1 slice of Toast.	Watercress.

Cut the tripe in small dice. Melt the margarine in a saucepan, add the chopped onion, the potatoes peeled and cut in dice, and the celery cut in fine shreds. Fry these until brown, then stir in the flour, and brown that also. Add the water slowly and stir until the soup thickens. Put in the tripe and season to taste. Cover, and simmer slowly for ½ hour. Pour in the milk, and add the leaves of the watercress well washed and finely chopped. Serve hot with sippets of toast.

Cowheel Hotchpotch

1 Cowheel.	1 small Cabbage.
3 tab. sps. Pearl Barley.	2 Onions or Leeks.
3 qrts. Cold Water.	Parsley and Herbs.
2 Carrots.	2 ozs. Butter or Drip'ng
1 Turnip.	Salt and Pepper.

Cut the cowheel into four pieces. Put it into a large saucepan with the cold water and the barley well washed. Grate down one of the carrots, put it aside in a little water, and chop all the rest of the vegetables very small. When the water boils, skim carefully, then add the prepared vegetables along with the fat, and a small bunch of herbs. Simmer all gently about 2 hours, then add the grated carrot and simmer ½ hour longer. Add seasoning and some chopped parsley at the last. Before serving the hotchpotch lift out the herbs, remove all flesh from the cowheel, cut it in small pieces, and return it to the saucepan.

Spanish Soup

1 Cowheel.	6 Potatoes.
1 lb. pickled Pork.	2 or 3 Sticks of Celery.
2 to 3 qts. Cold	A small bunch of
Water.	Herbs.
2 large Onions.	1 French roll.
2 small Cabbages.	Grated Cheese.
Some Pumpkin or Vegetable Marrow.	

Cut up cowheel and wash the pork. Put both into a large saucepan with the cold water, bring to the boil and skim well. Then add all the vegetables, prepared and cut in small pieces, using about 6 small pieces of pumpkin or marrow. Add also a small bunch of herbs, and cook all slowly until the pork is tender. When ready, remove the meat and season the soup to taste. Break up the French roll, put it in the tureen and grate some cheese over. Moisten with some of the liquor from the soup, place all the vegetables carefully on the bread, then add more liquor, and when the tureen is full, grate a little more cheese on the top. The pork can be served as a separate dish and eaten either hot or cold. If the soup is made in the morning, the pork could be served with parsley sauce and peas pudding for the midday meal, and the soup for supper, when the fat could be more easily skimmed off.

SECOND PRIZE

Tripe and Celery

2 lbs. Tripe.	1 pint Milk.
3 tab. sps. Onion.	1 bkfst. cupful diced
2 ditto Butter or	Celery.
Margarine.	Pepper and Salt.
1 ditto Flour.	

Cut the tripe into strips about 2 inches in length. Put these into a lined saucepan with the onion finely chopped and the butter or margarine. Cook them for 5 or 10 minutes, shaking the saucepan occasionally, and without allowing the contents to burn. Then add the milk, and when almost boiling, stir in the flour, which has been mixed to a paste with a little milk or water. When smoothly thickened, add salt and pepper to taste, and the celery, chopped or cut in dice. Simmer until the celery is tender, stirring occasionally, and serve garnished with sippets of toast.

Tripe à la Mode de Caen

2 lbs. Tripe.	3 Cloves, a sprig of
1 Cowheel.	Thyme and a Bay
2 Carrots.	Leaf.
2 or 3 Onions.	Pepper and Salt.
3 Leeks.	Water or Cider.

Cut the cowheel and tripe in small pieces and prepare the vegetables. Take a deep casserole, or stew-pot, and put in first a layer of the vegetables cut in slices, the cloves and herbs. Then put in some of the tripe and cowheel with a sprinkling of pepper and salt, more vegetables and so on. Cover with sliced leeks, and pour in enough water or cider to come fully half-way up the sides of the casserole. Put on a lid and cook slowly in the oven for 3 or 4 hours, or until all is well cooked. Remove the bones before serving and colour the gravy with a little caramel or brown sugar if desired. This is a very popular way of cooking tripe in France, and the result is very tasty.

Tripe a la Napolitaine

2 lbs. Tripe.	2 or 3 Tomatoes.
4 ozs. Naples Macaroni.	1 oz. Flour.
1 gill Boiling Water.	1 oz. Butter.
Seasoning.	1 pt. Milk.

Wash the macaroni and cut it in short lengths. Cut the tripe in small pieces, and peel and slice the tomatoes. Put all into a saucepan or earthenware casserole with the boiling water, and a seasoning of pepper and salt. Put on the lid and simmer slowly for ½ hour, or until the tripe and macaroni are

111

Stews and Fricassees

tender. Stir occasionally to prevent the macaroni sticking to the saucepan. Add the milk, and then the butter mixed smoothly with the flour. Stir until this thickens, and cook 5 minutes longer. Taste if sufficiently seasoned and serve very hot.

Tripe with Dumplings

1 lb. Tripe.
2 large Onions.
Salt and Pepper.
1 pint Water.
3 or 4 Potatoes.
1½ ozs. Beef Dripping or Bacon Fat.

DUMPLINGS.
¼ lb. Flour.
¼ teaspoonful Salt.
A little Milk.
2 ozs. Suet.
¼ teaspoonful Baking Powder.

Cut the potatoes and tripe into small pieces and skin and slice the onions very thinly. Put all into a large stewpan with the dripping and water, seasoning liberally with pepper and salt. Bring to the boil and simmer slowly ¾ of an hour.

To PREPARE THE DUMPLINGS.—Sieve the flour, salt and baking powder, add the suet finely chopped and mix all together. Moisten with a little milk, and make up into very small balls. Add these to the stew and cook 20 minutes longer.

Stewed Tripe with Mashed Potatoes

2 lbs. Honeycomb Tripe.
1½ pints Milk.
1 doz. small White Onions.
White Pepper and Salt.
2 Yolks of Eggs or 1 tab. sp. Cornflour.
Mashed Potatoes.
Chopped Parsley, Burnet or Chervil.

Cut the tripe in pieces about 2 ins. by 3 ins. Put it into a saucepan with the milk and stew it slowly, adding the onions peeled and scalded about ¼ hour before the tripe is ready. Add pepper and salt to taste. The onions should be tender but not broken. When ready strain off the milk and keep the tripe and onions warm. Put the milk into a small saucepan and thicken it with the yolks of eggs beaten with a little cold milk, or with the cornflour mixed to a smooth paste with milk. Taste the sauce and add more seasoning if necessary. Arrange some nicely mashed potatoes in a high pile in the centre of a hot dish. Stand the pieces of tripe round the base and the whole onions outside the tripe. Pour the sauce over the tripe and onions, leaving a mound of potatoes clear in the middle. Sprinkle this with chopped parsley, burnet or chervil, and serve very hot. This can be made quite a picturesque looking dish.

Tripe Stewed with Tomatoes

1 lb. Tripe.
1 lb. Tomatoes.
Cold Water.
Seasoning.
1 oz. Flour.
1 oz. Butter.
1 gill Milk.

Cut the tripe into small pieces, and place them in a clean saucepan with cold water to cover. Bring slowly to the boil. Place the tomatoes in boiling water for a minute or so, then lift them out and peel off the skins. Cut them in slices and add them to the tripe with pepper and salt to taste. Put on the lid and simmer for 20 minutes longer. Make a thickening by mixing the flour smoothly with the milk, add it to the stew and stir until boiling. Add the butter broken in small pieces at the last. Serve with toast or bread and butter.

Stewed Tripe with Onions

1 lb. Honeycomb Tripe.
2 Spanish Onions.
1 oz. Butter.
1 oz. Flour.
½ pint Milk.
Pepper and Salt.
A pinch of Nutmeg.
1 slice of Toast.

Cut the tripe in small pieces. Skin and scald the onions and cut them in quarters. Put onions into a saucepan cover with warm water and simmer slowly about 2 hours, or until tender. Then add the tripe and simmer for further ¼ hour. Mix the flour to a smooth cream with the milk and add to the contents of the saucepan. Stir until the flour thickens, add seasoning and the butter broken in small pieces. Cook all together for a few minutes and serve very hot garnished with sippets of toast.

NOTE.—The tripe may be stewed entirely in milk if desired ; it makes a whiter and more delicate stew.

Braized Tripe

1 lb. Tripe.
½ lb. lean Steak.
1 large Onion.
2 Carrots.
1 or 2 stalks of Celery.
A little Dripping.
Pepper and Salt.

Wipe the steak and cut it in small pieces. Melt the dripping in a stewpan, and when hot put in the steak and brown it on all sides. Then lift it out on to a plate. Cut the vegetables in pieces and place them at the bottom of the stewpan. Lay the steak and tripe (cut in pieces) on the top, and add seasoning to taste. Put on a tight fitting lid and cook slowly for 1 hour. No water is required, there will be sufficient moisture in the tripe and vegetables. Add no thickening, but serve the tripe when ready with a dish of nicely mashed potatoes.

Stewed Rabbit and Cowheel

1 Rabbit.
1 Cowheel.
3 or 4 Onions.
3 Cloves.
A little Parsley.
Cold Water.
1 tab. sp. Flour.
½ pint Milk.
1 oz. Butter.
Pepper and Salt.

Cut the rabbit into neat joints. Split the head and allow that and the neck to soak in salt and water for ½ an hour. Wash and dry the rabbit, place it in a stewpan with the cowheel cut in pieces and cover with cold water. Bring to the boil and skim carefully. Add the onions, cloves, and a few parsley stalks, cover and simmer slowly from 1½ to 2 hours or until tender. Lift out the rabbit, the cowheel and onion, arrange them on a hot dish and remove the cloves. Mix the flour gradually with the milk, add them to the liquid left in the saucepan, stir until boiling and season to taste. Put in the butter in small pieces, and when thoroughly blended pour over the meat.
A little chopped parsley may be added to the sauce.

Stewed Tripe de Luxe

2 lbs. Tripe.
Milk and Water.
1 Spanish Onion.
A sprig of Parsley.
Seasoning.
1 oz. Butter.
½ oz. Flour.
1 gill Cream.
Rind of ¼ Lemon.

Cut the tripe in pieces. Place it in a lined saucepan with equal parts of milk and water to cover. Add the onion cut in thin slices and the parsley. Put on the lid and simmer slowly for one hour. Mix the flour smoothly with the cream, and stir them into the tripe. Add also the thinly peeled rind of ¼ lemon, and seasoning to taste. Simmer slowly for another hour, remove the parsley and add the butter broken in small pieces just before serving. Serve with fingers of dry toast.

Tripe en Casserole

1 lb. Tripe.
¼ lb. Kidney.
¼ lb. Calf's Liver.
¼ tea sp. mixed Herbs.
A little Flour.
2 ozs. Dripping.
1 Carrot, 1 Turnip and 1 Onion.
Stock or Meat
Extract and Water.

Cut the tripe into small square pieces, and the kidney and liver into thin slices. Mix the flour with pepper, salt, and the herbs very finely powdered, and toss it in the tripe, liver and kidney, until all the pieces are coated. Melt the dripping in a casserole, put in the onion thinly sliced and fry it a golden brown. Add the carrot and turnip also sliced and the prepared meat. Fry all together for a few minutes and then pour off any superfluous fat. Add enough stock to barely cover the contents of the casserole, put on the lid, and stew very gently for 2 hours or longer. Add more seasoning if necessary, and serve in the casserole.

112

Stews and Fricassees

Lancashire and Yorkshire

1 lb. Tripe.	1 dessert sp. Flour.
3 medium sized Onions.	1 gill Milk.
1 tab. sp. Rice.	Pepper and Salt.
1 gill Water.	½ oz. Butter.
Yorkshire Relish.	

Cut the tripe in small pieces. Peel the onions and cut them in quarters, and wash the rice in several waters. Put these into a stewpan with the water, pepper and salt, bring to the boil and stir well. Then put on the lid and simmer until thoroughly cooked, stirring occasionally. Mix the flour smoothly with the milk and add them to the ingredients in the saucepan. Bring to the boil and cook for five minutes, stirring all the time. Add the butter just before dishing. Serve with a slice of hot buttered toast for each person, on hot plates, and sprinkled with Yorkshire Relish.

Tripe Olives

1 lb. Honeycomb Tripe.	½ pt. Stock or Water.
¼ lb. Bacon.	A small bunch of Herbs
2 small Onions.	1 oz. Butter.
1 dessert sp. Parsley.	1 oz. Flour.
Pepper and Salt.	A squeeze of Lemon Juice.

Cut the tripe into pieces about 2 inches wide and 3 inches long. Cut the bacon the same size and put a piece on each portion of tripe. Sprinkle with chopped onion, parsley, pepper and salt. Roll up and tie with a string, or narrow tape. Place the rolls in a stewpan, with a small sprig of thyme and marjoram, and stock to cover. Put on the lid and simmer gently for 2 hours. Then lift out the rolls on to a hot dish and remove the binding. Strain the stock in which they were cooked into a basin, and melt the butter in the pan. Mix in the flour, and then pour back the stock. Add a few drops of lemon juice, taste if sufficiently seasoned, and pour over rolls. Serve with a green vegetable.

Tripe and Cowheel Stew

3 lbs. Tripe.	A sprig of Thyme.
1 Cowheel.	2 or 3 Cloves.
2 large Carrots.	Seasoning.
3 Onions.	1 cupful Water.

Cut the tripe and cowheel into convenient sized pieces. Prepare the carrots and onions and cut them into thin slices. Now take a large stew-jar or casserole and put in first a layer of prepared vegetables with some of the tripe and cowheel on the top. Then put in more vegetables, more tripe and so on until all are in, being careful to finish with a layer of vegetables. A few pieces of celery may also be added, and sprinkle with pepper and salt. Pour the water over the top and then cover closely. Stand the jar in a saucepan of water and keep this slowly boiling until tender. Be careful to add fresh water from time to time in order to keep up the supply. When the stew is ready remove it from the saucepan, and let it stand for a short time before serving.

Cowheel Fricassee

1 Cowheel.	1 gill of Stock.
1 oz. Butter or Marg.	1 hard-cooked Egg.
1 oz. Flour.	Pepper and Salt.
1 gill Milk.	1 small Beetroot.

Stew the cowheel in enough water to cover it until quite tender. Then remove the bone and cut the cowheel in small pieces. Dish it up neatly and keep it warm. Melt the butter in a small saucepan, and stir in the flour until quite smooth. Pour in the milk and a gill of the water (or stock) in which the cowheel was cooked, and stir constantly until boiling. Chop the egg, add it to the sauce with seasoning to taste, and cook for a few minutes. Pour the sauce over the cowheel and garnish with neatly cut pieces of cooked beetroot.

Jugged Beef and Cowheel

1 Cowheel.	3 or 4 Cloves.
1 lb. Shoulder Steak.	Rind of ½ Lemon.
2 tab. sps. Flour.	1 blade of Mace.
Seasoning.	Hot Water.
2 ozs. Dripping or Bacon Fat.	1 glass Port Wine.
2 Onions.	Forcemeat Balls.
	Red Currant Jelly.

Cut steak and cowheel into small pieces. Roll them in flour seasoned with pepper and salt, then fry in the fat made smoking hot in a frying pan. When nicely browned put the pieces into an earthenware casserole with the onions, cloves, mace and grated lemon rind. Cover with warm water, and when it boils remove the scum. Simmer gently from 3 to 4 hours, or until thoroughly tender, add more seasoning if necessary, and the port wine 10 minutes before service. Serve hot with fried forcemeat balls and red currant jelly.

Cowheel with Parsley Sauce

2 Cowheels.	1½ ozs. Dripping or Butter.
1 Onion.	1½ ozs. Flour.
2 Cloves.	1 tab. sp. chopped Parsley.
2 Sticks of Celery.	
Water.	
Pepper and Salt.	

Cut the cowheels in four pieces and put them into a saucepan with cold water to cover. Add a little salt, bring to the boil and skim. Put in the onion stuck with the cloves, and the celery cut in small pieces. Cook 2 or 3 hours or until the pieces of heel are tender. The time will depend on the previous preparation. When ready, strain, remove the bones and cut the gelatinous pieces of heel into small pieces. Melt the dripping or butter in a stewpan and stir in the flour until smooth. Add 2 cupfuls of the liquid in which the heel was cooked and stir until boiling. Add parsley, seasoning and pieces of heel, and simmer all together for a few minutes. Dish up and serve very hot.

NOTE.—A little milk may be used for making the sauce, instead of some of the stock.

Cowheel with Piquant Sauce

1 Cowheel.	1 oz. Butter.
2 Onions.	1 oz. Flour.
A bunch of Sweet Herbs.	1 des. sp. chopped Pickles.
1 doz. Peppercorns.	Lemon.
Water.	Salt to taste.

Choose a cowheel weighing about 2 lbs. and cut it into four pieces. Put it into a stewpan with the onions cut in slices, the bunch of herbs, peppercorns, and a little salt. Cover with cold water, and boil very gently until the meat leaves the bones. Then strain through a sieve and reserve the stock. Now make a sauce. Melt the butter in a saucepan and let it brown. Add the flour and brown that also. Then pour on a pint of the stock, stir until boiling and skim if necessary. Cut the meat from the bones into small pieces and add it to the sauce, along with chopped pickles and any additional seasoning. Heat all gently and serve garnished with slices of lemon.

Aspic or Savoury Jelly

1 Cowheel.	4 Cloves.
5 pts. Cold Water.	1 blade of Mace.
1 Carrot.	1 gill Assorted Vinegars.
1 Onion.	1 gill Sherry.
1 Leek.	Whites and shells of 2 Eggs.
2 sticks Celery.	
A small bunch of Herbs.	1 Lemon.
20 Peppercorns.	1 tea sp. Salt.

Cut the cowheel in pieces. Put it into a large saucepan with the cold water, bring to the boil and skim carefully. Then add the vegetables, prepared and cut in pieces, bunch of herbs and spices, and boil all gently for 5 or 6 hours. Strain through a hair sieve and leave until cold. Now remove all fat from the stock, return it to a clean saucepan, and if not sufficiently stiff, add a little gelatine. Add also the yellow rind and juice of the lemon, a little brown chilli and tarragon vinegar mixed, sherry, whites and shells of eggs and salt to taste. Whisk the contents of the saucepan over the fire until almost boiling. Remove whisk and let the jelly boil up. Then draw to one side, cover and when settled strain through a hot jelly cloth until running clear. Stand until cold and use as a garnish for cold meat, salad, etc.

Mincemeat

1 lb. Honeycomb Tripe.	½ lb. Candied Peel.
1 lb. Currants.	½ lb. Suet.
½ lb. Sultana Raisins.	2 tea sps. Mixed Spice.
½ lb. Valencia Raisins.	½ ditto Ginger.
1 lb. Apples.	Rind and juice of 2 Lemons.
1 lb. Sugar.	
1 or 2 glasses of Sherry.	

Pies and Hot Pots

Chop the tripe very finely and put it into a basin. Clean the currants and sultanas, and stone and chop the Valencia raisins. Peel, core and chop the apples, shred and chop the suet, and chop the candied peel. Mix all these ingredients with the tripe, and add sugar, spices, and the grated rind and strained juice of the lemons. Mix until thoroughly blended, and add the wine at the last. Put into pots and tie down to exclude air. Use for making mince-pies.

Children enjoy the appetising variety of dainty U.C.P. Recipes — and it is so good for them because of its nutritious body-building qualities and digestive simplicity.

114

Pies and Hot Pots

Cut up the meat and cowheel. Put them into a stewpan with cold water to cover, a little salt and the onion stuck with cloves. Simmer slowly for 2 or 3 hours or until tender. Strain, remove the bones, and cut the flesh of the cowheel into small pieces. Put the beef and cowheel into a deep baking dish, or pie-dish, and pour over them some of the liquor in which they were cooked, well seasoned with pepper, salt, and a little ketchup or Worcester sauce. The dish must not be quite full, and the liquid should barely cover the meat. Make a suet pastry with the above ingredients and roll to the size of the dish. Lay it carefully on the top of the meat, cover with a high lid and cook in a good oven for ¾ hour, or until the pastry is done. Serve very hot.

Small Picnic Pies

Cowheel.   Seasoning.
1 lb. Stewing Beef.   Pastry.

Cut the cowheel in four pieces and put it into a saucepan. Wipe the meat, cut it in pieces, and add it to the cowheel. Cover all with cold water, bring to the boil, and skim if necessary. Simmer until the beef is tender and the bones come away easily from the cowheel. Strain, reserving the liquor. Remove the bones, chop the meat, but not too small, season it well and let it cool. Make some plain pastry and line small greased pie tins, fill them with the minced meat and put on a pastry cover. Press the edges well together, and make a hole in the top. Bake in a hot oven from 15 to 20 minutes. Remove the fat from the stock, warm a little of it until liquid, add pepper and salt, and pour some into each pie through the hole in the top. This will jelly as the pies cool. These pies are very convenient for carrying out-of-doors.

Tripe Pasties

Line some greased saucers, or large patty tins, with some short crust rolled out rather thinly. For the filling, chop finely some cooked tripe, add to it some chopped parsley, a little grated nutmeg, pepper and salt. Moisten with beaten egg or piquant sauce, and fill up the lined tins or saucers with this mixture. Cover with rounds of pastry, wetting the edges where the two pieces join. Press well together and make a hole in the centre. Brush over with a little milk or beaten egg, and bake in a good oven until the pastry is nicely browned and thoroughly cooked. Garnish the pasties with a little parsley, and serve them either hot or cold.

NOTE.—A little cooked and chopped ham or bacon may be added to the mixture if desired.

Delicious Luncheon Pie

	PASTRY.
1 Cowheel.	3 ozs. Lard.
1 lb. Shoulder Steak.	1 tea sp. Salt.
Pepper and Salt.	¼ teasp. Baking Pwdr.
½ lb. Flour.	Boiling Water.

Place the cowheel in a saucepan with boiling water to cover and a little salt, and let it boil until the bones can be removed easily. Then put the steak and cowheel through the mincing machine. Place the mince in the saucepan with the water in which the cowheel was cooked, season with pepper and salt and simmer gently for 2 hours. Strain off any liquid and let the mince cool.
Make some pastry with the above ingredients. Rub the lard into the flour, add the salt and baking powder, form into a paste with boiling water and roll out. Line a round greased cake tin with this (one with a loose bottom is best), and fill in with the meat. Put on a lid of pastry, wetting the edges where it joins, trim round with a pair of scissors and brush over with a beaten egg. Make a small hole in the lid, and bake the pie in a hot oven about 1 hour, or until the pastry is cooked and nicely browned. When ready fill up through the hole with some of the melted gravy that was strained from the meat. Set aside until cold and the jelly is stiff, then turn out and garnish with parsley.

Beef and Cowheel Pasty

	PASTRY.
1 large Cowheel.	
½ lb. Shin of Beef.	½ lb. Dripping.
1 quart Water.	1 tea sp. Salt.
Pepper and Salt.	½ tea sp. Baking Pwdr.
½ lb. Flour.	Cold Water.

Cut the cowheel and beef in pieces. Put them into a stew-jar with the water, salt and pepper to taste, and cook in the oven until fairly tender. Then strain, reserving the liquor. Remove the bones and put the beef and cowheel through the mincer. Add more seasoning if necessary and moisten with a little of the liquor. Make a simple pastry with the above ingredients, divide it in two, and roll out each piece into a round. Grease a large plate and line it with one piece of pastry. Put in the mince, wet round the edges and cover with the other round of pastry. Press the two together and trim round with a pair of scissors. Mark round the edges neatly, make a hole in the centre, and ornament with the pastry trimmings. Brush over with a little milk or beaten egg, and bake in a good oven for ½ hour, or until the pastry is well cooked and nicely browned. Serve hot or cold.

Cowheel and Rabbit Pie

1 Cowheel.	Cold Water.
1 Rabbit.	Seasoning.
1 large Onion.	Pie-crust.

Cut the cowheel in pieces free from bone. Wash and clean the rabbit and cut it in neat joints. Put these into a pie-dish with seasoning of pepper and salt. Peel the onion, and put it in whole, with the top cut in the form of a cross. Then cover the contents of the dish with cold water, put a plate or lid on the top and cook in a moderate oven until nearly tender. Now remove the lid, grease the edge of the dish, and when the meat is nearly or quite cold, cover with a good pie-crust. Bake until brown and thoroughly cooked, and serve with boiled potatoes.

NOTE.—A few slices of streaky bacon may be added to the pie, if desired.

Tripe Hot Pot

1 lb. Tripe.	A little Flour.
1 lb. Spanish Onions.	Seasoning.
2 lbs. Potatoes.	1 tab. sp. Beef
Stock.	Dripping.

Cut the tripe in small pieces, and coat them with a little flour. Prepare the potatoes and onions, and cut them both into slices. Take a deep baking dish, or hot pot dish, and grease it with good dripping. Put in the different ingredients in layers, seasoning with pepper and salt, and making the last layer a thick one of sliced potatoes. Pour in enough stock to come half-way up the sides of the dish and put the rest of the dripping in small pieces on the top. Cover with a lid and cook in a good oven 1 hour or longer. Remove the cover and brown the top before serving. Serve in the dish.

NOTE.—A few sliced tomatoes may be added to the above ingredients if desired.

MONOTONY in meals can be avoided by dainty meals contrived with U.C.P. Tripe and Cowheels

Cold Dishes and Salads

A MEMORABLE MEAL

'On a summer evening in the shadow of a famous castle, my hostess declared she had prepared for me a famous dish. It was indeed a dish of tripe— for an epicure.

I am no gourmand, but the memory of that meal lingers still. The sunset, the castle, the lake, the glimmering candles, and that dish of tripe."

Tripe Loaf

1½ lbs. Honeycomb Tripe. ¼ lb. cooked Ham. Seasoning.

Simmer the tripe in a small amount of water until quite tender. Then take a square tin or pie-dish, rinse it out with cold water and put some thin slices of boiled ham at the bottom. Next put in some tripe, seasoning it with pepper and salt, then more ham, and so on in layers until the vessel is full. Pour in some of the liquid in which the tripe was cooked, press with a plate, and put aside until cold. Turn out when required and serve cut in slices with salad and mint sauce.

Cowheel and Tripe Brawn

2 lbs. Honeycomb Tripe.   Seasoning.
1 large Cowheel.   Water.
1 lb. Lean Beef.

Cut the tripe and beef in medium sized pieces. Put all into a saucepan with cold water to cover, and simmer from 6 to 8 hours. Skim when necessary and be careful the liquid does not reduce too much. Then strain, and remove the bones. Cut the meat, tripe, and cowheel small, or chop them roughly, and then return them to the liquor. Season carefully, and pour into wetted moulds or basins to set.

Cowheel Mould

1 Cowheel.
¼ lb. Ham or Bacon.   1 des. sp. chopped Parsley.
2 hard-cooked Eggs.   Grated Lemon Rind.   Pepper and Salt.

Cook the cowheel in water to cover, and strain, reserving the liquor. Remove the bones, and cut the flesh of the cowheel into thin slices. Trim the ham or bacon, and cut that also in small pieces. Mix the cowheel and ham together and sprinkle them with pepper, salt, a little grated rind and the chopped parsley. Take a plain mould and rinse it out with cold water, leaving it wet. Cut the eggs in slices or sections, and arrange a few pieces at the bottom of the mould. Then fill nearly to the top with the prepared meat and the rest of the eggs. Pour in some of the liquor in which the cowheel was cooked, cover with greased paper and bake in a moderate oven 1 hour. Add more liquor if the mould is not quite full, and put aside until cold and firm. This makes a very good breakfast or luncheon dish.

Potted Beef and Cowheel

1 Cowheel.
1 lb. Shin or Neck of   Water.
  Beef.   Seasoning.

Cut the cowheel and meat in pieces. Place them both in a saucepan and just cover with cold water. Bring to the boil and simmer gently for 3 hours or longer, until the contents are perfectly tender. Then strain, remove all the bones, and chop the meat and cowheel together. Return the mince to the saucepan with the liquor, and add pepper, salt, a little grated nutmeg, and a pinch of powdered cloves. Bring to the boil again, stirring frequently. Pour into moulds that have been rinsed out with cold water, and stand in a cool place until set. Turn out when required, and serve plain or with salad. This is delicious.

NOTE.—Sometimes a little vegetable is added to flavour the meat, but the mixture will not keep so well. Pork or mutton may be used in place of beef.

Cowheel and Rabbit Mould

1 Cowheel.
1 Rabbit.   1 hard-boiled Egg.
Cold Water.   Seasoning.

Cut up the rabbit and cowheel. Put them into a large stew-jar or stew-pot, and season the pieces well with pepper and salt. Barely cover with cold water, put on a lid, and stew in a moderate oven for 3 or 4 hours. Then strain, take out all the bones and cut the meat into neat pieces. Ornament a plain mould with the egg cut in pieces, and put in the prepared meat without disturbing the decoration. Fill up with the liquid and put the mould in a cool place to set. Serve cold with salad.

Potted Tripe

¼ lb. Tripe.   Pepper and Salt.
1 tea sp. Tomato   ¼ tea sp. made
  Sauce.   Mustard.
A pinch of Nutmeg.   A little Butter.
A pinch of Mace.

Put the tripe once or twice through a mincing machine until reduced to a paste. Add the spice, tomato sauce and seasoning, mixing all well together. Press into small pots, and run a little melted butter over the top to exclude the air. This is excellent for sandwiches.

Galantine of Tripe

1 lb. Tripe.   1 Onion.
¼ lb. Fat Bacon.   1 Egg.
¼ lb. Breadcrumbs.   Seasoning.
1 tab. sp. chopped   Meat Glaze or Bread-
  Parsley.   crumbs.

Cut the tripe and bacon in pieces, and put them both through the mincing machine. Put the mince into a basin and add to it the onion finely chopped, breadcrumbs, parsley and seasoning. Mix well and bind together with a beaten egg. Form into a roll, using a little flour, tie up in a scalded pudding cloth, and steam for 2 hours. Then press between two dishes until cold. Remove the cloth, coat the galantine with liquid meat glaze, or brush it over with a little melted butter, and sprinkle with brown breadcrumbs. Serve cold cut in slices, with pickled beetroot or salad.

Tripe with Beetroot and Potato Salad

1 lb. Tripe.   1 tea sp. chopped
½ doz. cold Potatoes.   Parsley.
1 or 2 Beetroots.   2 hard-cooked Yolks.
1 small Onion.   2 tab. sps. Salad Oil.
Seasoning.   1 tab. sp. Ketchup.
  1 tab. sp. Vinegar.

Cut the tripe in small pieces. Slice the potatoes, and peel and slice the beetroots. Arrange these artistically in a salad dish, sprinkling the ingredients with the onion finely chopped. Pour the dressing over and sprinkle lightly with chopped parsley.

TO MAKE THE DRESSING.—Sieve or chop the yolks and mix them in a basin with salt, pepper, a little made mustard, and a pinch of sugar. Add the oil gradually, and when thoroughly blended pour in the ketchup and vinegar. This is an excellent dressing for serving with tripe. The whites of the eggs should be cut in shreds and mixed with the salad ingredients.

Fried Dishes

Pickled Tripe

1 lb. Tripe.	3 pickled Onions.
Pepper and Salt.	3 pickled Walnuts.
1 cupful Breadcrumbs.	A little Vinegar.
A little Gravy.	Sippets of Toast.

Cut the tripe into convenient sized pieces, and season them with pepper and salt. Now dip each piece of tripe first into gravy and then into breadcrumbs. Chop the pickles and then arrange the tripe and pickles in layers, in a greased pie-dish. Pour a little vinegar from the pickles over the top, place the dish in a moderate oven, and cook until thoroughly hot. Serve with sippets of toast arranged neatly on the top.

Tripe Salad

1 lb. Tripe.	1 hard-cooked Egg.
1 Lettuce.	Salad Dressing.
1 Tomato.	

Cut the tripe into fine shreds. Wash and dry a nice lettuce and cut the tomato and egg in quarters. Pile the tripe in the centre of a glass dish or salad bowl and pour over it some salad dressing. Arrange the lettuce in a border round and garnish with alternate pieces of egg and tomato.

To MAKE THE DRESSING.—Mix in a small basin a little pepper, salt and made mustard. Add 2 tablespoonfuls of salad oil gradually, and when these are blended add 1 tablespoonful of malt vinegar. A little sugar may also be added.

A Summer Day's Feast

1 lb. Tripe.	FOR THE SAUCE.
½ lb. Tomatoes.	Horseradish.
1 crisp Lettuce.	Pepper and Salt.
2 hard-boiled Eggs.	A pinch of Sugar.
Boiled Beetroot.	2 tab. sps. Cream or Salad Oil.
	1 dess. sp. Vinegar.

Place a glass—such as a champagne glass, or a small sugar basin with a leg on it—in the centre of a large shallow salad dish. In the salad dish arrange the tripe cut in pieces, then alternate row or layers of tomato, lettuce, beetroot, and hard-boiled eggs. The lettuce should be lightly broken with the fingers, the tomato, beetroot and eggs cut in slices, and the different ingredients prettily arranged. Then fill up the centre glass with horseradish sauce and place a salad spoon and fork at the side.

To MAKE THE SAUCE.—Grate the horseradish and put it into a basin, add the seasoning and then moisten with the cream or salad oil, and lastly the vinegar.

Fried Tripe

1 lb. Honeycomb Tripe.	A little Flour.
2 tab. sps. Salad Oil.	1 Egg.
1 tab. sp. chopped Onion.	Breadcrumbs.
1 tab. sp. Lemon Juice.	Seasoning.

Cut the tripe into neat pieces. Mix on a plate the oil, lemon juice, chopped onion, pepper and salt. Lay the pieces of tripe in this and let them soak for ½ hour or so. Then drain them on paper, and coat the pieces lightly with flour. Beat up an egg on a plate with a little water and seasoning, and have ready some breadcrumbs. Egg and breadcrumb the pieces of tripe next, then fry them in boiling fat until prettily browned. Drain, and serve piled up in a dish hot, garnished with parsley. Potato chips or fried tomatoes may be served separately.

Tripe Fritters

1 lb. Tripe.	BATTER.
1 des. sp. chopped Parsley.	¼ lb. Flour.
	A pinch of Salt.
Pepper and Salt.	1 Egg.
A little Lemon Juice.	A small teacupful
Fat for Frying.	tepid Water.

Cut the tripe in pieces about 2 inches square, and have it as dry as possible. Sprinkle the pieces with chopped parsley, pepper, salt, and a little lemon juice.

To MAKE the BATTER.—Sieve the flour and salt into a basin and make a well. Add the yolk of egg and then the tepid water by degrees. Stir and beat well with a wooden spoon. When perfectly smooth let the batter stand for 1 hour if possible, as this gives time for the flour to swell.

Just before using stir in the white of egg beaten to a stiff froth. Dip each piece of tripe into the batter and fry in hot fat to a golden brown. Drain on paper and serve hot, garnished with parsley.

Bubble and Squeak

1 lb. Honeycomb Tripe.	Cold mashed Potatoes.
1½ ozs. Dripping or Butter.	1 tea sp. Vinegar.
1 small Onion.	Pepper and Salt.

Melt the fat in a frying pan and put in the tripe cut in thin slices. Fry quickly until lightly browned on both sides, then remove the tripe and keep it hot. Have the onion finely chopped or cut in very thin shreds, put it next into the frying pan and cook until brown. Put in a little more if necessary, and add some cold mashed potatoes well seasoned with pepper and salt. Stir until thoroughly hot and add the vinegar, if liked. Arrange the potato mixture neatly on a hot dish, and place the slices of tripe on the top.

A Good Breakfast Dish

Take as many nice slices of Tripe as required, and sprinkle them with a little white pepper and salt. Roll each slice of tripe in a very thin slice of bacon, and large enough to cover it. Dip these into beaten egg, and then into breadcrumbs. Fry in boiling fat to a nice brown colour, and serve very hot, garnished with parsley.

Fried Cowheel

1 Cowheel.	1 Egg.
1 des. sp. Flour.	1 tea sp. chopped Parsley.
Seasoning.	
Frying Fat.	Grated Lemon Rind.
	Breadcrumbs.

Cook the cowheel until tender, remove the bones, and press the pieces of flesh between two plates until cold. Then cut them in neat pieces. Season the flour with pepper and salt, and dip each piece of heel into the mixture, coating it very lightly. Beat up the egg on a plate with the parsley and a little grated lemon rind, and prepare some fine breadcrumbs. Next egg and breadcrumb the pieces of heel and fry them in boiling fat until a golden brown. Drain on paper, and serve piled up and garnished with parsley. Some good brown gravy or tomato sauce may be served separately. Mashed potatoes would make a good accompaniment.

Tripe and Ham Cutlets

½ lb. Tripe.	1 des. sp. chopped Parsley.
3 ozs. cooked Ham.	
1 oz. Butter.	A pinch of Nutmeg.
1 tea sp. Grated Onion.	1 Yolk of Egg.
	Pepper and Salt.
1 tab. sp. Flour.	A little Flour.
1 teacupful Milk.	Egg and Breadcrumbs.

Mince the ham finely and cut the tripe into small pieces. Melt the butter in a saucepan, put in the onion and cook it a few minutes. Then mix in the flour and add the milk. Stir until boiling and cook for a minute or two. Add the parsley, ham, tripe and seasoning, and mix well. Remove the saucepan from the fire and add the yolk of egg. Turn the mixture on to a plate, smooth it over with a knife, and let it cool. Then divide it into eight pieces, and form each of these into cutlet shape, using a little flour. Egg and breadcrumb them and reshape. Then fry them in boiling fat until a golden brown. Drain and put a small piece of macaroni into the narrow end of each to represent the bone of the cutlet. Serve up neatly and garnish with parsley. A little tomato sauce may be served separately.

Fried Dishes

Fried Liver and Tripe

½ lb. Honeycomb Tripe.
¼ lb. Calves' or Sheep's Liver.
1 or 2 Onions.
A little Flour.
2 ozs. Dripping.
Chopped Parsley.

Wash and dry the liver and cut it in thin slices. Cut the tripe in strips and coat them both with a little flour. Peel and slice the onions thinly, and fry them in the dripping, until brown and tender. Lift them out, keep them hot, aud then fry the liver and tripe. Serve on the top of the onions, pour a little brown sauce or gravy over, and sprinkle lightly with chopped parsley. This makes a very tasty and somewhat novel dish.

Grilled Tripe with Potato Chips

1 lb. Tripe.
1 tab. sp. chopped Parsley.
1 tab. sp. chopped Onion.
1 des. sp. Lemon Juice.
2 tab. sps. melted Butter.
Pepper and Salt.
Breadcrumbs.
Potato Chips.

Mix together the parsley, onion, lemon juice and seasoning and stir in the melted butter. Cut the tripe into square pieces, dip them into the mixture and then coat with breadcrumbs. Grill on both sides until brown, and serve with hot potato chips. Tomato or any other favourite sauce may be served separately.

Mock Sweetbreads

1 lb. Tripe.
1 Egg.
Grated Lemon Rind.
Breadcrumbs.
Seasoning.
½ lb. Mushrooms.
2 ozs. Butter or Marg.
A squeeze of Lemon Juice.
Mashed Potatoes.

Cut the tripe in small squares. Beat up a small egg on a plate and add to it a little pepper, salt, and grated lemon rind. Dip each piece of tripe into this, coating it well, and then toss in finely sieved breadcrumbs. Press the crumbs on with the hands and leave to dry for a few minutes on a tin covered with kitchen paper. Meanwhile, wash and peel the mushrooms and cut them in pieces. Melt the butter in a small saucepan, put in the mushrooms with seasoning, and a squeeze of lemon juice, cover closely and cook for ten minutes. Heat about 2 cupfuls of mashed potatoes, pile them in the centre of a hot dish, and make a hollow in the centre. Fry the tripe, or mock sweetbreads, in boiling fat, until a golden brown. Drain on the paper, and then arrange round the potatoes. Put the mushrooms in the hollow of the potatoes and pour some brown gravy round.

Tripe Cutlets with Baked Beans

1 lb. Tripe
1 Egg.
Pepper and Salt.
Breadcrumbs.
1 tin of Baked Beans.
A pinch of Cayenne.

Cut the tripe into pieces about 3 inches long by 2 inches wide. Beat up the egg on a plate and add seasoning, and have some finely made breadcrumbs on a piece of paper. Egg and breadcrumb the pieces of tripe carefully, then fry them in boiling fat until a golden brown colour on both sides. Drain them on paper and arrange them in the centre of a hot dish. Make the beans smoking hot and pour them round. Serve with mashed potatoes.

Tripe Rissoles

1 lb. mixed Tripe.
2 cupfuls Mashed Potatoes.
1 tab. sp. chopped Parsley.
1 des. sp. chopped Onion.
1 Yolk of Egg.
A little Milk.
A little Flour.
Egg and Breadcrumbs.
Fat for Frying.

Use a mixture of tripe, black and white. Mince it very finely and mix it in a basin with an equal amount of mashed or sieved potato. Season rather highly and add the parsley and onion, both finely chopped. Bind with the yolk of egg and a little milk if necessary. Form the mixture into small balls of equal size, using a little flour, then coat them with beaten egg aud breadcrumbs and fry in boiling fat until a pretty brown colour. Drain and serve garnished with parsley. Some well-washed celery, served in a glass. is a good accompaniment to rissoles.

Tripe Sausages

1 lb. Tripe.
½ lb. Beef Steak.
½ lb. Beef Suet.
½ lb. Breadcrumbs.
A little Flour.
The rind of ½ Lemon.
6 Sage Leaves.
A little Nutmeg.
Pepper and salt.

Cut the tripe into small pieces. Wipe the steak and cut it in pieces, removing any skin. Then put the tripe and beef through a mincing machine, mincing them very finely. Put the mince into a basin and add to it the breadcrumbs and the suet finely chopped. Then the sage leaves, finely powdered, the grated lemon rind and other seasoning. Form into rolls like sausages and coat them with flour. Melt some dripping in a frying pan, when smoking hot put in the sausages and fry them slowly until brown on all sides and thoroughly cooked. Drain and serve with mashed potatoes, and with or without gravy.

Tripe, quickly prepared

1 lb. Tripe.
2 ozs. Margarine or Butter.
1 or 2 Onions.
1 des. sp. chopped Parsley.
A little Vinegar.
Pepper and Salt.

Peel the onions and cut them in very thin slices. Heat the fat in a frying pan and cook the onion slices until brown. Add the tripe, cut in small pieces, and cook a few minutes longer. Add parsley, pepper, salt and vinegar, mix well and serve very hot with dry toast.

NOTE.—Any remains of cooked tripe can be reheated in this way.

Tripe for Breakfast

1 lb. Tripe.
¼ lb. Ham or Bacon.
4 Tomatoes.

Fry the ham or bacon and the tomatoes in a frying pan, and when sufficiently cooked lift them out on to the serving dish and keep them warm. Then fry the tripe in the bacon fat, cooking it for a few minutes on each side. Serve the tripe on the top of the bacon, with the tomatoes round the sides. This makes a delicious meal.

A Tasty Tripe Dish

1 lb. Tripe.
1 gill Milk.
1 gill Water.
1 Egg.
Breadcrumbs.
Pepper and Salt.
1 cupful each of Onions, cooked carrots and Potatoes.
A little Dripping.
1 Meat Cube.
1 tea sp. Cornflour.

Cut tripe in pieces about 5 inches long and 3 inches broad. Put these into a saucepan with the milk and water, and cook them gently until tender. Then lift out the pieces of tripe, let them dry. Meanwhile have the vegetables cut in slices. Make the dripping hot in a frying pan, and first put in the thinly sliced onion and fry it a golden brown, then add the carrot and potato and fry them until brown also. Season with pepper and salt, turn all into a dish and keep warm. Now egg and breadcrumb the pieces of tripe, fry them a golden brown and then arrange them neatly on the top of the vegetables. Mix the cornflour with the liquid left from stewing the tripe, turn into a saucepan, add the meat cube and stir until boiling. Season and strain round tripe.

Baked Tripe

¼ lb. Honeycomb	Liquor from the Tripe.
Tripe.	White Pepper and Salt.
4 thin slices of Bread.	A little Butter or
1 Egg.	Dripping.

Cut the tripe into small pieces, and soak the bread with a little of the tripe liquor. Grease a pie-dish and lay in one slice of the bread, then some of the tripe, another slice of bread and the remainder of the tripe. Cover entirely with the last two slices of bread, making them fit in neatly. Beat up the egg with the seasoning and a small teacupful of the tripe liquor, and pour this over the bread. Put a few small pieces of butter or dripping on the top, and bake in a good oven about 20 minutes. Serve very hot. This is light and nourishing.

Baked Tripe (another way)

1½ lbs. Tripe.	Butter or Dripping.
2 cupfuls Breadcrumbs.	2 Eggs.
3 or 4 onions.	Seasoning.

Cut the tripe into pieces and line the bottom of a greased pie-dish with it. Sprinkle over this a few breadcrumbs with seasoning, then a layer of onions, which have been sliced and fried. Then put in some more tripe and breadcrumbs, and so on, repeating the layers until the dish is full. The top layer should be breadcrumbs. Beat up the eggs with a little of the liquid in which the tripe was cooked, and strain over the top. Place in the oven, and bake ¾ hour. Serve in the same dish. Boiled Spanish Onions and melted butter may be served separately.

Stuffed Vegetable Marrow

1 Vegetable Marrow.	1 tea sp. Gravy.
¼ lb. Tripe.	1 Yolk of Egg.
4 Onions.	Seasoning.
2 tea sp.s Parsley.	1 tea sp. chopped
2 or 3 tab. sps. Bread-	Onion.
crumbs.	Browned Bread-
	crumbs.

Boil the four onions in salted boiling water until tender, drain and chop them finely. Add to them the tripe, finely chopped, breadcrumbs and chopped parsley. Season to taste and bind together with the yolk of an egg and a little gravy if necessary. Choose a large fresh marrow, cut out a wedge, and remove all the seeds and inside pith. Fill with the above ingredients and replace the wedge. Put the marrow in a baking tin or dish with some hot dripping and sprinkle it with some browned breadcrumbs and the chopped onion. Bake from ½ to 1 hour, basting now and again with the dripping. When ready, lift carefully on to a hot dish and serve with brown or tomato sauce.

Lady Glenconner tells a story of one of her children who mounted a table at his birthday party and made a little speech. "I hope you will eat my birthday cake with savage gusto," he said. Children and grownups eat dainty U.C.P. meals, with *gusto*, although perhaps not with *savage* gusto.

Gateau of Tripe

Line a greased tin with nicely seasoned mashed potatoes, reserving enough to cover the top. Fill up the lined tin with alternate layers of tripe cut in small pieces peeled and sliced tomato, and small sprigs of cooked cauliflower. Moisten each layer with well-seasoned white sauce and cover entirely with mashed potatoes. Bake in a good oven for ½ hour until the potato is well browned on the sides as well as the top. Turn out, garnish with parsley, and serve with white or tomato sauce.

This makes a very good luncheon dish.

A Tasty Supper Dish

2 lbs. honeycomb Tripe.	3 ozs. grated Cheese.
2 tea sps. Bovril.	Mashed Potatoes.
3 ripe Tomatoes.	1 tea sp. chopped
	Parsley.

Cut the tripe in pieces, cover with cold water, and simmer gently for 1 hour. Add the Bovril and seasoning and stir until thoroughly mixed. Scald the tomatoes, remove the skins, and cut them in thin slices. Place the tripe in a greased pie-dish with the tomatoes on the top. Sprinkle with the cheese and spread a layer of mashed potatoes over the top. Place in a moderately hot oven until the top is a golden brown, sprinkle with parsley, and serve hot.

Tripe, Stuffed and Roasted or Mock Duck

2 lbs. Black Tripe.	1 Egg.
1 lb. Onions.	Seasoning.
½ lb. Sausages.	A little Dripping.
1 cupful Breadcrumbs.	1 des. sp. Flour.
1 des. sp. Parsley.	½ pt. Stock or Gravy.

Boil the onions until tender, drain and chop them finely. Remove the skins from the sausages and add them to the onions with the breadcrumbs, parsley finely chopped, and seasoning. Mix all together and moisten with the egg well beaten. Choose the tripe in one large piece, spread it out on a board, lay in the stuffing, roll up and tie with string. Place some dripping in a roasting tin, make it hot in the oven and lay in the tripe. Roast for ¾ hour, or until well cooked, basting frequently. When ready lift the tripe on to a hot dish and remove the string. Pour away most of the fat from the tin, sprinkle in the flour and stir over the fire until brown. Then pour in the stock or gravy (½ pt. of water and a meat cube may be used) and bring to the boil, stirring all the time. Add seasoning if necessary, remove any scum, and strain round the tripe.

Baked and Stuffed Tripe

Mock Goose

2 lbs. Black Tripe.
2 cupfuls Breadcrumbs.
1 cupful chopped Onion.
1 tea sp. Sage.
Lemon Rind.
Seasoning.
A little Dripping.
3 or 4 slices fat Bacon.
Mashed Potatoes.
1 des. sp. Flour.
2 cupfuls stock or Gravy.

Choose the tripe in one piece, Spread it out on a board. Then prepare a stuffing. Peel and scald one or two onions and chop them finely. Add to them the breadcrumbs, the sage finely powdered, a little grated or chopped lemon rind, pepper and salt. Mix all together, adding a little milk if necessary to bind. Spread this stuffing over half of the tripe, place a few small pieces of dripping on the top, and cover with the other half. Sew the edges together, and place the tripe in a greased baking tin with a few slices of fat bacon on the top.

Bake in a moderate oven about 2 hours, basting the tripe occasionally. When ready place the mock goose on a hot dish, and pile nicely mashed potatoes round it. Make some brown sauce by adding the flour to the fat in the baking tin and stirring until brown. Pour in the stock or gravy and stir until boiling. Skim, season to taste and serve separately.

Tripe with Fresh Herrings

1 lb. Tripe.
4 fresh Herrings.
Seasoning.
Lemon Juice.
1 des. sp. Flour.
1 tab. sp. Parsley.
A little Butter or Dripping.

Cut the tripe in small squares, season with pepper and sprinkle with lemon juice. Clean and bone the herrings, and rub with salt. Grease a large baking dish and put in half the tripe. Place two herrings opened flat and with the skin side uppermost on the top. Sprinkle with flour and parsley, repeat the layers, and put a few small pieces of fat on the top. Bake in a good oven for 30 minutes. this makes a delicious and economical dish.

Tripe and Liver Roll

1 lb. Tripe.
½ lb. Liver.
1 cupful Breadcrumbs.
1 tab. sp. chopped Parsley.
Grated Lemon Rind.
A pinch of Thyme.
Beaten Egg.
1 pt. stock or Gravy. Seasoning.

Choose the tripe in one large piece. Wash and stew the liver until tender, then mince it finely and mix it with the breadcrumbs, parsley, lemon rind, thyme and seasoning. Moisten with some beaten egg and form into a roll. Place in the centre of the tripe, roll up and stitch with a needle and cotton. Place the roll in a greased baking dish and pour the stock or gravy round. Cover and bake in a moderate oven for 1 hour. To serve, place the roll on a hot dish, remove the cotton, thicken the gravy if preferred, season to taste, and pour it round.

Tripe Steak

1 lb. honeycomb Tripe.
1 tea sp. chopped Parsley.
1 des. sp. chopped Onion.
1 teacupful White Sauce.
1 ditto Boiled Rice.
Seasoning.
1 des sp. Lemon Juice.

Keep the tripe in one piece and lay it in a greased baking dish. Sprinkle with the onion, parsley, lemon juice and seasoning. Mix the rice and white sauce together, and cover the tripe with this. Bake in a moderate oven for 20 minutes and serve hot with green peas or new potatoes.

Tripe and Chestnut Roll

2 lbs. Tripe.
1 lb Chestnuts.
½ lb. Breadcrumbs.
1 tab. sp. fine Sago.
A little grated Lemon. Rind.
Pepper and Salt.
Brown Gravy.

SUET CRUST.
1 lb. Flour.
6 ozs. Suet.
1 tea sp. Salt.
½ teasp. Baking Pwdr.
Cold Water.

Buy the tripe in one piece if possible. Boil the chestnuts until tender, remove the shells and mash them. Mix them with the breadcrumbs, seasoning, and a little grated lemon rind. Bind all together with the sago, which has been soaked in a little hot water. Put this stuffing in the centre of the tripe and roll it up. Then make the Suet Crust. Sieve the flour, salt and baking powder into a basin, add the suet finely chopped and mixed together. Form into a paste with cold water and roll out. Put the tripe roll in the centre, fold the crust over it and seal it in securely. Place the roll on a greased tin and bake in a good oven from 1½ to 2 hours. Serve with brown sauce or gravy in a sauce boat.

Tripe, Stuffed and Steamed

1 lb. honeycomb Tripe.
½ lb. Stewing Beef.
¼ lb. Ox Kidney.
A little Flour.
Brown Gravy.
1 Onion.
1 tab. sp. minced Parsley.
Seasoning.
2 ozs. Dripping.

Wipe the steak, wash and dry the kidney, and cut them both in small pieces. Sprinkle them with flour, pepper and salt. Melt the dripping in a frying pan and fry the meat and kidney until brown. Spread the tripe out on a board, and sprinkle with seasoning. Spread over it the steak and kidney and sprinkle with the parsley and onion finely minced. Roll up and stitch with a large needle and white thread, sewing up the ends. Wrap in a scalded and floured pudding cloth and steam for 4 hours. Make some gravy in the pan in which the meat was fried. Dish up the tripe when ready and pour the gravy over. Decorate with slices of lemon and tomato. Serve with mashed potatoes.

Curried Tripe

1 lb. Tripe.
1 large Onion.
1 oz. Dripping or Butter.
1 Apple.
1 des. sp. Curry Pwdr.
Seasoning.
½ pt. Stock or Water.
1 des. sp. Cornflour.
1 tab. sp. Cocoanut.
1 cupful Milk.
½ tea sp' Lemon Juice.
Boiled Rice.

Melt the butter or dripping in a stewpan, when hot put in the onion finely chopped and fry it until brown. Add the apple also chopped, and the curry powder, and mix well. Pour in the stock or water, add the tripe cut in small pieces and simmer until tender, about 1 hour. Mix the cornflour smoothly with the milk, add it to the curry, and stir until the sauce thickens. Add the dessicated cocoanut, lemon juice and seasoning to taste. A tablespoonful of cream may also be added. Serve with a dish of carefully boiled rice.

TO BOIL RICE FOR CURRY.—Wash ¼ lb. unpolished rice in several waters. Then throw it into a saucepan with plenty of fast-boiling water slightly salted. Cook from 15 to 20 minutes, or until tender, stirring frequently with a fork. Pour into a sieve or strainer and wash all the starch out of the rice by pouring water through it, hot if possible. This will separate the grains. Then put the rice in the oven to dry and keep warm. Serve in a separate dish from the curry.

Tripe à l'Indienne

1 lb. Tripe.
1 pt. White Sauce.
1 tea sp. Curry Pwdr.
1 Yolk of Egg.
1 oz. Butter.
Brown Breadcrumbs.

Cut the tripe, which must be very tender, into small pieces. Make the sauce and put the tripe into it. Add the curry powder which has been mixed smoothly with a little cold water. Heat slowly, add the beaten yolk, and stir over the fire a few minutes longer. Grease a pie-dish with some of the butter, put the mixture into it, cover the top with a layer of breadcrumbs, and put the remainder of the butter in small pieces on the top. Place in a hot oven from 10 to 15 minutes, and serve very hot.

Kedgeree of Tripe

½ lb. Tripe.
½ lb. Rice.
1 oz. Dripping or Butter.
1 tea sp. Onion.
2 hard-boiled Eggs.
Seasoning.
2 tab. sps. Worcester Sauce.
2 tea sps. chopped Parsley.

Wash the rice, cook it in plenty of fast-boiling water until tender, drain and dry it well. Chop the tripe finely and chop the onion. Melt the fat in a saucepan, put in the onion and cook it carefully. Then add the tripe and cook it over the fire for a few minutes. Next stir in the rice and season to taste with pepper, salt, a little made mustard and the Worcester sauce, and make all thoroughly hot. Separate the yolks from the

Curries and Savouries

whites of the hard-boiled eggs. Shred the whites and add them to the mixture, and rub the yolks through a wire sieve. Pile up the mixture neatly on a hot dish, and decorate with alternate lines of yolk of egg and chopped parsley, or according to fancy.

Tripe and Egg Scramble

½ lb. honeycomb Tripe.	1 oz. Butter.
2 Eggs.	Pepper and Salt.
1 des. sp. chopped Parsley.	3 slices fried Bread, or hot Buttered Toast.

The tripe must be tender. Chop it finely Break the eggs into a basin and beat them slightly. Then season with pepper and salt, add the tripe and parsley and stir all together. Melt the butter in a saucepan, add the tripe and egg mixture, and stir until sufficiently cooked, like scrambled eggs. Serve on the fried bread or toast. This is a good dish for breakfast or high tea.

Tripe Rarebit

1 lb. Tripe.	1 tea sp. Curry Pwdr.
3 small Onions.	Pepper and Salt.
2 Tomatoes.	1 des. sp. Vinegar.
1 oz. Butter or Dripping.	Toasted or Fried Bread.

Cut the tripe into small pieces about 1 inch square. Peel and slice the onions very thinly. Peel the tomatoes and cut them also in slices. Melt the fat in a frying pan, when hot put in the sliced onions and fry them until brown. Then add the tripe and tomatoes, and sprinkle with pepper and salt. Mix the curry powder smoothly with the vinegar, add them to the other ingredients. Cook over the fire for ½ hour longer, stirring frequently. Serve very hot on slices of toast or fried bread. This is very tasty and delicious.

Tripe Omelet

½ lb. Tripe.	1 des. sp. Flour.
3 eggs.	½ tea sp. Dried Herbs
3 tab. sps. Milk.	Pepper and Salt.
1 small Onion.	1½ ozs. Butter.

Put the flour and milk into a basin, and blend them smoothly together. Break in the eggs, and add the herbs finely powdered, tripe minced, pepper and salt. Beat the ingredients together with a wire whisk until they are thoroughly incorporated. Then melt the butter in an omelet or frying pan, put in the onion very finely chopped and cook it a minute or two. Pour in the mixture and keep shaking the pan over the heat until the omelet is set, and nicely browned at the bottom. Fold over, transfer to a very hot dish, and serve at once.

Tripe Toast

1 lb. Seam Tripe.	1 cupful Milk.
2 ozs. Butter.	Seasoning.
1 des. sp. Flour.	Buttered Toast.

Cut the tripe in small pieces. Put the butter, flour and milk into a saucepan, and stir over the fire until they boil. Add the tripe, season to taste, and heat gently. Prepare some hot buttered toast, and arrange the tripe neatly on the top.
This is a quickly made and appetising dish for supper.

Cowheel Curry

1 Cowheel.	1 des. sp. Rice Flour.
1 small Onion.	½ pt. Stock.
1 Apple.	1 tea sp. Chutney.
1 oz. Butter.	Salt and Pepper.
1 tea sp. Curry Pwdr.	Boiled Rice.
½ a Lemon.	

Have the cowheel cooked until tender, remove the bone, and cut it in small pieces. Slice a small onion or shallot and fry it in the butter until brown. Then add the apple peeled and chopped, the curry powder and rice flour. Cook these over the fire for a minute or two longer, then add the stock and stir until boiling. Put in the pieces of cowheel with the chutney and seasoning, and simmer slowly for 1 hour. Serve garnished with slices of lemon, and some well boiled rice on a separate dish.

Savoury Tripe

1½ lbs. Tripe.	1 pt. Stock or Water.
½ lb. Tomatoes.	Seasoning.
½ lb. Mushrooms.	2 tab. sps. Bread-
1½ ozs. Beef Dripping.	crumbs.
1 tab. sp. Flour.	A little grated Cheese.

Wipe the tomatoes and remove the stalks and peel and wash the mushrooms. Cut both in convenient sized pieces. Melt the dripping in a saucepan, when hot fry the mushrooms and tomatoes for a few minutes, and then lift them out on to a plate. Add flour to the fat left in the pan and let it brown slightly. Pour in the stock (or water with a little meat extract may be used) and stir until boiling. Add pepper and salt if necessary. Cut the tripe into pieces and lay them in a greased pie dish or casserole, cover with the mushrooms and tomatoes and strain the brown sauce over. Sprinkle with the breadcrumbs and grated cheese. Cook and brown in a moderate oven about 30 minutes. Serve with potatoes, preferably fried.

Savoury Tripe and Potatoes

1½ lbs. Tripe.	1 gill Milk.
1 oz. Butter.	¼ lb. Cheese.
Seasoning.	Mashed Potatoes.
1 oz. Flour.	

Steam the tripe (do not boil) until tender, then place it in a greased pie-dish or baking dish. Put the liquid from the tripe into a small saucepan, add the milk and flour mixed smoothly together, and stir until boiling. Add most of the cheese grated, and season to taste. Simmer until the cheese is melted, pour over the tripe, and sprinkle the remainder of the cheese on the top. Brown in the oven or under the grill, and serve with a good dish of mashed potatoes.

Tripe and Macaroni

1 lb. Tripe.	½ pt. Milk.
2 ozs. Macaroni.	Pepper and Salt.
1 oz. Butter.	2 tab. sps. grated
1 oz. Flour.	Cheese.
	1 slice of Toast.

Boil the macaroni in salted water until tender. Drain and cut it in ½-inch pieces. Make a white sauce with the butter, flour and milk. Put in the macaroni, cheese and seasoning, and heat slowly. Cut the tripe into small pieces, add it to the other ingredients and, when thoroughly hot and saturated with the sauce, serve garnished with sippets of toast.

Scalloped Cauliflower and Tripe

1 lb. Tripe.	½ pt. White Sauce.
1 Cauliflower.	¼ lb. grated Cheese.
Seasoning.	

Cut the tripe in small pieces. Wash and trim cauliflower, soak it in cold water for an hour, then steam it for 30 minutes, or until tender. Now break it apart into small pieces and arrange it, along with the tripe in a greased baking or grating dish. Heat the sauce, add to it most of the cheese, and season rather highly with pepper, salt and a little made mustard. Pour this sauce over the cauliflower and tripe, sprinkle the remainder of the cheese on the top, and brown in the oven or under the grill.

Mock Crab

½ lb. Tripe.	A little Butter.
2 new laid Eggs.	Mustard and Vinegar.
Pepper and Salt.	Hot Buttered Toast.

Mince the tripe finely. Boil the eggs until set and remove the shells. Put them into a basin with a little butter and break them up with a fork. Add the tripe and season with pepper and salt. A little made mustard and vinegar may also be added, or these can be served separately. Arrange on hot buttered toast, and make hot in the oven. This can also be served cold.

Tripe with Poached Eggs

Take a pound of honeycomb tripe and cut it in pieces the size of a small saucer. Put these pieces into a saucepan or casserole with a gill of milk, pepper and salt, and let them cook gently until tender, but not broken. When ready, lift the pieces carefully on to a hot dish and place a poached egg on the top of each. Add to the liquid left in the saucepan 1 teaspoonful of flour mixed smoothly with 2 tablespoonfuls of milk. Stir until boiling and cook for a minute or two. Taste if sufficiently seasoned and then strain round the eggs. Serve with dry toast. This makes an excellent dish for supper or high tea.

Specially for Invalids

Tripe Soup for an Invalid

¼ lb. Tripe.   1 cooked Onion.
½ oz. Butter.   ½ pt. Milk.
½ oz. Flour.   Seasoning.
½ pt. Tripe Liquor.   A small slice of Toast.

Stew the tripe and onion in water until tender, then strain and keep the liquor. Cut the tripe in small dice, and chop the onion. Melt the butter in a saucepan, add the flour and mix until smooth. Pour in ½ pint tripe liquor, and stir until boiling. Then add the tripe and onion and simmer gently for ½ hour. Add the milk and seasoning and bring to the boil. The yolk of an egg may also be added if desired. Serve with fingers of thin toast.

Tripe with White Sauce

½ lb. honeycomb Tripe.   A little Butter.
1 gill Milk.   Seasoning.
1 des. sp. Flour.

Cut the tripe into neat pieces. Put it into a double cooker with the milk and butter. Steam it for 2 hours, being careful to keep plenty of water in the under saucepan. Blend the flour with a little cold milk, and add to the contents of the saucepan, stirring all the time, and season to taste. Serve with fingers of dry toast.

NOTE.—If a double cooker is not available the tripe may be cooked in a jar, placed in a saucepan of boiling water.

Milk Jelly with Cowheel

½ Cowheel.   1 inch Cinnamon Stick.
1 pt. new Milk.   ¼ lb. loaf Sugar.
Rind of 1 Lemon.

Put the ½ cowheel into a jar with the milk. Add the very thinly peeled rind of a lemon, cinnamon and sugar. Cover closely and bake in the oven for 4 hours. Strain and leave to cool, then remove all fat from the top and use as required. This may be served with cream, fruit juice or a little stewed fruit.

NOTE.—A little wine may be added after straining.

Nourishing Tripe

½ lb. Tripe.   1 Egg.
½ teacupful Milk.   White Pepper and Salt.

Cut the tripe into three or four pieces. Put it into a casserole or lined saucepan with the milk, season to taste, and simmer very slowly until tender, about ¾ of an hour. Then lift on to a dish. Beat up the egg, add it to the liquid in the saucepan, and stir over the fire until thick but without allowing it to boil. Pour over the tripe garnish with parsley, and serve hot with toast.

NOTE.—If the liquid in the saucepan has reduced very much, add cold milk to make up the original amount.

Lemon Jelly from Cowheel

1 Cowheel.   2 inches Cinnamon
4 or 5 pts. Water.   Stick.
6 ozs. Loaf Sugar.   1 gill Sherry.
3 Cloves.   Rind of 2 lemons.
Whites and shells of   1 gill Lemon Juice.
   2 Eggs.

Cut the cowheel in four pieces, then put it into a saucepan with 4 or 5 pints of fresh cold water. Put on the lid and simmer slowly about 6 hours, until all the goodness is extracted from the heel and the liquid is reduced to half the original quantity. Strain through a fine seive or cloth and leave to cool. Next day this stock should be a stiff jelly. Remove all fat from the top and turn it into a clean saucepan. Add the sugar, cloves, cinnamon and sherry. Wipe two lemons and peel the rind of them very thinly. Add this to the other ingredients along with a gill of strained lemon juice, the whites of eggs, and the shells washed and crushed. Stand the saucepan over the fire and whisk the contents until almost boiling. Then let them boil up to the top of the pan. Draw gently to one side, cover and stand for ten minutes. Heat a jelly bag or cloth with boiling water, and strain the jelly through it into a basin. If the first cupful is cloudy pour it through a second time. It should be clear and bright. Cover and stand in a warm place until all has run through. Keep in a cold place and use as required.

NOTE.—A little orange juice may be used along with the lemon, and the sherry may be omitted.

Calves' Feet and Beef Jelly

2 Calves' Feet.   1 glass Port Wine.
¼ lb. lean Beef.   Pepper and Salt.
Cold Water.

Cut the feet and beef into small pieces and put them in a stewing jar. Add seasoning, and just cover with cold water. Put on a lid and stew slowly in the oven, or in a saucepan of boiling water, about 3 hours. When sufficiently cooked, strain, add the wine, and leave to set. This is very strengthening for an invalid.

Steamed Tripe

½ lb. honeycomb Tripe.   1 tea sp. Flour.
1 teacupful Milk.   Pepper and Salt.
½ oz. Butter.

Cut the tripe in small pieces and put it between two greased plates. Stand these over a saucepan of boiling water and steam for 40 minutes. Then make a little sauce with the butter, flour and milk, season it lightly and cook it well. Lift the tripe on to a serving dish and pour the sauce over. Serve with fingers of thin toast.

ABOVE is a miniature of a beautifully-printed showcard which is supplied to all retailers selling U.C.P. guaranteed pure products. U.C.P. Tripe and Cowheel can be obtained throughout Lancashire and the North from all retailers exhibiting the above Showcard and the U.C.P. Oval Red Sign.

OTHER LOCAL TITLES

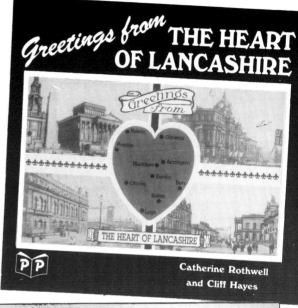

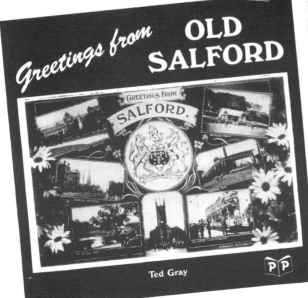

OTHER LOCAL TITLES

SONGS OF
A Lancashire Warbler

by
Lowell Dobbs

Hoo seet mi heart gooin' back an' forrit,
  Thumpin' like a facthry mule-
Then hoo spun her charms areawnd it
  Like silk areawnd a spool.

£4.95

If you have enjoyed this book...
look out for...

RON & MARLEEN FREETHY

Also coming shortly...

"Getting to Know
THE LAKE DISTRICT"

NORTHERN CLASSIC REPRINTS

NORTHERN CLASSIC REPRINTS

The Manchester Man

(Mrs. G. Linnaeus Banks)

Re-printed from an 1896 illustrated edition — undoubtedly the finest limp-bound edition ever. Fascinating reading, includes Peterloo. Over 400 pages, wonderfully illustrated.

ISBN 1 872226 16 7 £4.95

Poems & Songs Of Lancashire

(Edwin Waugh)

A wonderful quality reprint of a classic book by undoubtedly one of Lancashire's finest poets. First published 1859 faithfully reproduced. Easy and pleasant reading, a piece of history.

ISBN 1 872226 27 2 £4.95

The Manchester Rebels

(W Harrison Ainsworth)

A heady mixture of fact and fiction combined in a compelling story of the Jacobean fight for the throne of England. Manchester's involvement and the formation of the Manchester Regiment. Authentic illustrations.

ISBN 1 872226 29 9 £4.95

The Dock Road

(J. Francis Hall RN)

A seafaring tale of old Liverpool. Set in the 1860s, with the American Civil War raging and the cotton famine gripping Lancashire. Period illustrations.

ISBN 1 872226 37 X £4.95

Hobson's Choice (the Novel)

(Harold Brighouse)

The humorous and classic moving story of Salford's favourite tale. Well worth re-discovering this enjoyable story. Illustrated edition. Not been available since 1917, never before in paperback.

ISBN 1 872226 36 1 £4.95

The Lancashire Witches

(W. Harrison Ainsworth)

A beautifully illustrated edition of the most famous romance of the supernatural.

ISBN 1 872226 55 8 £4.95

THE STORIES
AND TALES SERIES

Stories and Tales Of Old Merseyside
(Frank Hird, edited Cliff Hayes)

Over 50 stories of Liverpool's characters and incidents PLUS a
booklet from 1890 telling of the city's history, well illustrated.
ISBN 1 872226 20 5   £4.95

Stories & Tales Of Old Lancashire
(Frank Hird)

Over 70 fascinating tales told in a wonderful light-hearted fashion.
Witches, sieges and superstitions, battles and characters all here.
ISBN 1 872226 21 3   £4.95

Stories and Tales Of Old Manchester
(Frank Hird, edited Cliff Hayes)

A ramble through Manchester's history, many lesser known stories
brought to life, informative yet human book. Over 50 stories.
ISBN 1 872226 22 1   £4.95

Stories Of Great Lancastrians
(written Frank Hird)

The lives of 24 great men of the county, told in easy reading style.
Complete with sketches and drawings, a good introduction to the
famous of Lancashire and Manchester. John Byrom, Arkwright, Tim
Bobbins, Duke of Bridgewater.
ISBN 1 872226 23 X   £4.95

More Stories Of Old Lancashire
(Frank Hird)

We present another 80 stories in the same easy, readable style, very
enjoyable, great. With special section for Preston Guild 1992.
ISBN 1 872226 26 4   £4.95

Have you seen . . .
LANCASHIRE 150
YEARS AGO

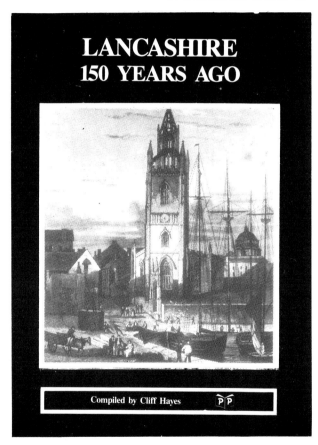

A great addition to the collection
of any lover of Lancashire's
history